Hockey
League

Official Rules

1994-95

M&S

National Hockey League Official Rules 1994-95

Printed in Canada.

Design, production by:
Dan Diamond and Associates, Inc.
194 Dovercourt Road
Toronto, Ontario M6J 3C8
416/531-6535 Fax 416/531-3939

Distributed in Canada by:
McClelland & Stewart Inc.
The Canadian Publishers
481 University Avenue
Toronto, Ontario M5G 2E9
905/940-8855 Fax 905/940-3642

Published in the United States of America by:
Triumph Books
644 South Clark Street
Chicago, Illinois 60605
312/939-3330 Fax 312/663-3557

The National Hockey League
1251 Avenue of the Americas, New York, New York 10020-1198
1800 McGill College Avenue, Suite 2600, Montreal, Quebec H3A 3J6
75 International Boulevard, Suite 300, Toronto, Ontario M9W 6L9

NATIONAL HOCKEY LEAGUE

OFFICIAL RULES

TABLE OF CONTENTS

NOTE: "Commissioner" in these playing rules shall mean Commissioner of the National Hockey League or any League Officer designated by him to perform duties and exercise authority set out in these rules.

ALPHABETICAL INDEX

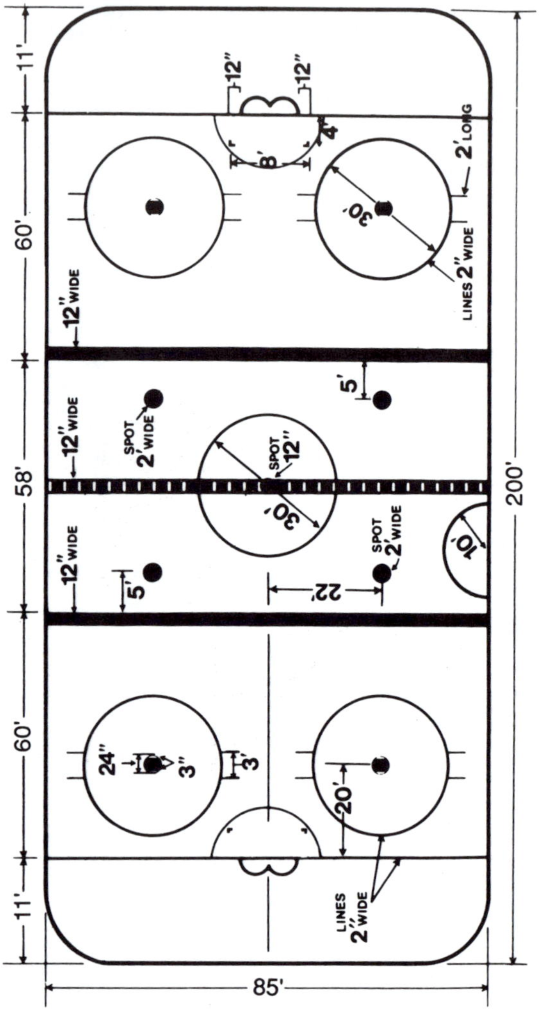

OFFICIAL DIMENSIONS OF RINK SURFACE

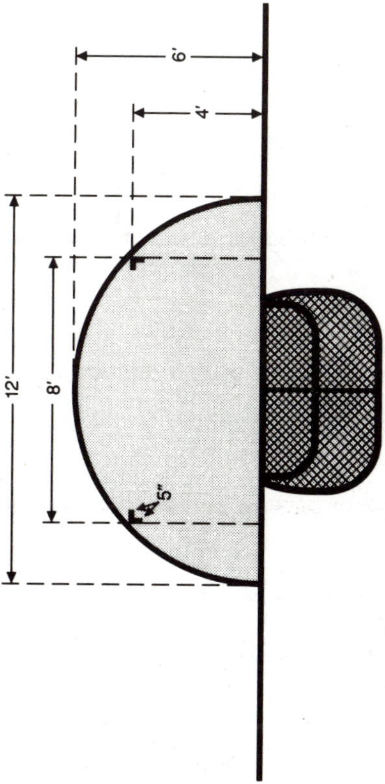

DETAIL OF GOAL CREASE

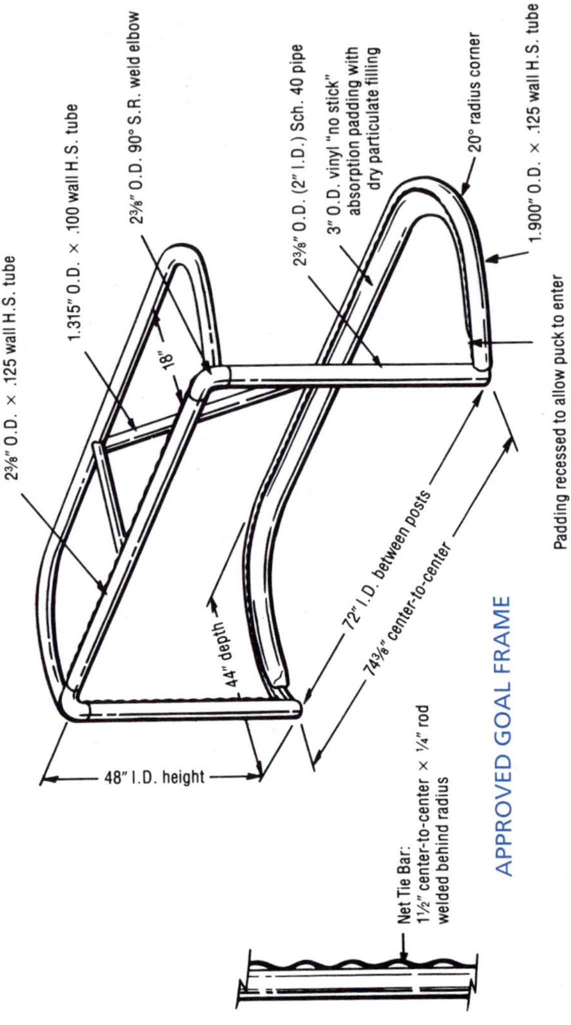
2³/₈" O.D. × .125 wall H.S. tube
1.315" O.D. × .100 wall H.S. tube
2³/₈" O.D. 90° S.R. weld elbow
18"
2³/₈" O.D. (2" I.D.) Sch. 40 pipe
3" O.D. vinyl "no stick" absorption padding with dry particulate filling
20° radius corner
1.900" O.D. × .125 wall H.S. tube
Padding recessed to allow puck to enter
44" depth
72" I.D. between posts
74³/₈" center-to-center
48" I.D. height
Net Tie Bar:
1½" center-to-center × ¼" rod
welded behind radius
APPROVED GOAL FRAME

RULES GOVERNING THE GAME OF ICE HOCKEY

SECTION ONE – THE RINK

Rule 1. Rink

The game of "Ice Hockey" shall be played on an ice surface known as the "RINK".

(NOTE) There shall be no markings on the ice except as provided under these rules without the express written permission of the League.

Rule 2. Dimensions of Rink

(a) The official size of the rink shall be two hundred feet (200') long and eighty-five feet (85') wide. The corners shall be rounded in the arc of a circle with a radius of twenty-eight feet (28').

The rink shall be surrounded by a wooden or fibreglass wall or fence known as the "boards" which shall extend not less than forty inches (40") and not more than forty-eight inches (48") above the level of the ice surface. The ideal height of the boards above the ice surface shall be forty-two inches (42"). Except for the official markings provided for in these rules, the entire playing surface and the boards shall be white in color except the kick plate at the bottom of the board which shall be light blue or light yellow in colour.

Any variations from any of the foregoing dimensions shall require official authorization by the League.

(b) The boards shall be constructed in such manner that the surface facing the ice shall be smooth and free of any obstruction or any object that could cause injury to players.

All doors giving access to the playing surface must swing away from the ice surface.

All glass or other types of protective screens and gear to hold them in position shall be properly padded or protected. Protective glass shall be required in front of the penalty benches to provide for the safety of the players on and off the ice. All equipment used to hold the glass or screens in position shall be mounted on the boards on the side away from the playing surface.

Rule 3. Goal Posts and Nets

(a) Eleven feet (11') from each end of the rink and in the center of a red line two inches (2") wide drawn completely across the width of the ice and continued vertically up the side of the boards, regulation goal posts and nets shall be set in such manner as to remain stationary during the progress of a game. The goal posts shall be kept in position by means of flexible pegs affixed in the ice or floor.

Where the length of the playing surface exceeds two hundred feet (200'), the goal line and goal posts may be placed not more than fifteen feet (15') from the end of the rink.

(b) The goal posts shall be of approved design and material, extending vertically four feet (4') above the surface of the ice and set six feet (6') apart measured from the inside of the posts. A cross bar of the same material as the goal posts shall extend from the top of one post to the top of the other.

(c) There shall be attached to each goal frame a net of approved design made of white nylon cord which shall be draped in such manner as to prevent the puck coming to rest on the outside of it.

A skirt of heavy white nylon fabric or heavyweight white canvas shall be laced around the base plate of the goal frame in such a way as to protect the net from being cut or broken. This skirt shall not project more than one inch (1") above the base plate.

(NOTE) The frame of the goal shall be draped with a nylon mesh net so as to completely enclose the back of the frame. The net shall be made of three-ply twisted twine (0.130 inch diameter) or equivalent braided twine of multifilament white nylon with an appropriate tensile strength of 700 pounds. The size of the mesh shall be two and one-half inches (21/2") (inside measurement) from each knot to each diagonal knot when fully stretched. Knotting shall be made as to ensure no sliding of the twine. The net shall be laced to the frame with medium white nylon cord no smaller in size than No. 21.

(d) The goal posts and cross bar shall be painted in red and all other exterior surfaces shall be painted in white.

(e) The red line, two inches (2") wide, between the goal posts on the ice and extended completely across the rink, shall be known as the "GOAL LINE".

Rule 4. Goal Crease

(a) In front of each goal, a "GOAL CREASE" area shall be marked by a red line two inches (2") in width.

(b) The goal crease shall be laid out as follows: A semi-circle six feet (6') in radius and two inches (2") in width shall be drawn using the center of the goal line as the center point. In addition, an 'L'-shaped marking of five inches (5") in length (both lines) at each front corner will be painted on the ice.

The location of the 'L'-shaped marking is measured by drawing an imaginary four foot (4') line from the goal line to the edge of the semi-circle. At that point, the 'L' may be drawn. (See diagram on page 9.)

(c) The goal crease area shall include all the space outlined by the crease lines and extending vertically four feet (4') to the level of the top of the goal frame.

(d) The complete goal area, which includes the crease and to the base of the goal (to the back of the net) shall be painted a light blue colour. (Note: use paint code PMS 298.)

Rule 5. Division of Ice Surface

(a) The ice area between the two goals shall be divided into three parts by lines, twelve inches (12") in width, and blue in colour, drawn sixty feet (60') out from the goal lines, and extended completely across the rink, parallel with the goal lines, and continued vertically up the side of the boards.

(b) That portion of the ice surface in which the goal is situated shall be called the "DEFENDING ZONE" of the team defending that goal; the central portion shall be known as the "NEUTRAL ZONE", and the portion farthest from the defended goal as the "ATTACKING ZONE".

(c) There shall also be a line, twelve inches (12") in width and red in colour, drawn completely across the rink in center ice, parallel with the goal lines and continued vertically up the side of the boards, known as the "CENTER LINE". This line shall contain at regular interval markings of a uniform distinctive design which will easily distinguish it from the two blue lines... the outer edges of which must be continuous.

Rule 6. Center Ice Spot and Circle

A circular blue spot, twelve inches (12") in diameter, shall be marked exactly in the center of the rink; and with this spot as a center, a circle of fifteen feet (15') radius shall be marked with a blue line two inches (2") in width.

Rule 7. Face-off Spots in Neutral Zone

Two red spots two feet (2') in diameter shall be marked on the ice in the neutral zone five feet (5') from each blue line. The spots shall be forty-four feet (44') apart and each shall be a uniform distance from the adjacent boards.

Rule 8. End Zone Face-off Spots and Circles

(a) In both end zones and on both sides of each goal, red face-off spots and circles shall be marked on the ice. The face-off spots shall be two feet (2') in diameter. Within the face-off spot, draw two parallel lines three inches (3") from the top and bottom of the spot. The area within the two lines shall be painted red, the remainder shall be painted white.

The circles shall be two inches (2") wide with a radius of fifteen feet (15') from the center of the face-off spots. At the outer edge of both sides of each face-off circle and parallel to the goal line shall be marked two red lines, two inches (2") wide and two feet (2') in length and three feet (3') apart.

(b) The location of the face-off spots shall be fixed in the following manner:

Along a line twenty feet (20') from each goal line and parallel to it, mark two points twenty-two feet (22') on both sides of the straight line joining the center of the two goals. Each such point shall be the center of a face-off spot and circle.

Rule 9. Players' Benches

(a) Each rink shall be provided with seats or benches for the use of players of both teams and the accommodations provided including benches and doors shall be uniform for both teams. Such seats or benches shall have accommodation for at least fourteen persons of each team, and shall be placed immediately alongside the ice, in the neutral zone, as near to the center of the rink as possible with doors opening in the neutral zone and convenient to the dressing rooms.

Each players' bench should be twenty-four feet (24') in length and when situated in the spectator area, they shall be separated from the spectators by a protective glass of sufficient height so as to afford the necessary protection for the players. The players' benches shall be on the same side of the playing surface opposite the penalty bench and should be separated by a substantial distance.

(NOTE) Where physically possible, each players' bench shall have two doors opening in the neutral zone and all doors opening to the playing surface shall be constructed so that they swing inward.

(b) No one but players in uniform, the Manager, Coach and Trainer shall be permitted to occupy the benches so provided.

(NOTE) One non-uniformed player shall be permitted on the players' bench in a coaching capacity. He must be indicated on the Roster Sheet submitted by the Coach to the Referee or Official Scorer prior to the start of the game in accordance with Rule 15 – Players in Uniform.

Rule 10. Penalty Bench

(a) Each rink must be provided with benches or seats to be known as the "PENALTY BENCH". These benches or seats must be capable of accommodating a total of ten persons including the Penalty Timekeepers. Separate penalty benches shall be provided for each team and they shall be situated on opposite sides of the Timekeeper's area, directly across the ice from the players' benches. The penalty bench(es) must be situated in the neutral zone.

(b) On the ice immediately in front of the Penalty Timekeeper's seat there shall be marked in red on the ice a semi-circle of ten feet (10') radius and two inches (2") in width which shall be known as the "REFEREE'S CREASE".

(c) Each Penalty Bench shall be protected from the spectator area by means of a glass partition which shall not be less than five feet (5') above the height of the boards.

Rule 11. Signal and Timing Devices

(a) Each rink must be provided with a siren, or other suitable sound device, for the use of Timekeepers.

(b) Each rink shall be provided with some form of electrical clock for the purpose of keeping the spectators, players and game officials accurately informed as to all time elements at all stages of the game including the time remaining to be played in any period and the time remaining to be served by at least five penalized players on each team.

Time recording for both game time and penalty time shall show time remaining to be played or served.

The game time clock shall measure the time remaining in tenths of a second during the last minutes of each period.

(c) Behind each goal, electrical lights shall be set up for the use of the Goal Judges. A red light will signify the scoring of a goal and a green light will signify the end of a period or a game.

(NOTE) A goal cannot be scored when a green light is showing.

Rule 12. Police Protection

All clubs shall provide adequate police or other protection for all players and officials at all times.

The Referee shall report to the Commissioner any failure of this protection observed by him or reported to him with particulars of such failure.

SECTION TWO – TEAMS

Rule 13. Composition of Team

(a) A team shall be composed of six players on the ice who shall be under contract to the Club they represent.

(b) Each player and each goalkeeper listed in the line-up of each team shall wear an individual identifying number at least ten inches (10") high on the back of his sweater and, in addition, each player and goalkeeper shall wear his surname in full, in block letters three inches (3") high, across the back of his sweater at shoulder height.

All players of each team shall be dressed uniformly with approved design and colour of their helmets, sweaters, short pants, stockings and skates.

Altered uniforms of any kind, i.e. velcro inserts, over-sized jerseys, etc. will not be permitted. Any player or goalkeeper not complying with this rule shall not be permitted to participate in the game.

Each Member Club shall design and wear distinctive and contrasting uniforms for their home and road games, no parts of which shall be interchangeable except the pants.

Rule 14. Captain of Team

(a) One Captain shall be appointed by each team, and he alone shall have the privilege of discussing with the Referee any questions relating to interpretation of rules which may arise during the progress of a game. He shall wear the letter "C", approximately three inches (3") in height and in contrasting colour, in a conspicuous position on the front of his sweater.

In addition, if the permanent Captain is not on the ice, Alternate Captains (not more than two) shall be accorded the privileges of the Captain. Alternate Captains shall wear the letter "A" approximately three inches (3") in height and in contrasting colour, in a conspicuous position on the front of their sweaters.

(NOTE) Only when the captain is not in uniform, the Coach shall have the right to designate three Alternate Captains. This must be done prior to the start of the game.

(b) The Referee and official Scorer shall be advised prior to the start of each game, of the name of the Captain of the team and the Alternate Captains.

(c) Only the Captain, when invited to do so by the Referee, shall have the privilege of discussing any point relating to the interpretation of rules. Any Captain or player who comes off the bench and makes any protest or intervention with the officials for any purpose must be assessed a misconduct penalty in addition to a minor penalty under Rule 42(b) – Abuse of Officials.

A complaint about a penalty is NOT a matter "relating to the interpretation of the rules" and a minor penalty shall be imposed against any Captain or other player making such a complaint.

(d) No playing Coach or playing Manager or goalkeeper shall be permitted to act as Captain or Alternate Captain.

Rule 15. Players in Uniform

(a) At the beginning of each game, the Manager or Coach of each team shall list the players and goalkeepers who shall be eligible to play in the game. Not more than eighteen players, exclusive of goalkeepers, shall be permitted.

(b) A list of names and numbers of all eligible players and goalkeepers must be handed to the Referee or Official Scorer before the game, and no change shall be permitted in the list or addition thereto shall be permitted after the commencement of the game.

i) If a goal is scored when an ineligible player is on the ice, the goal will be disallowed.

ii) The ineligible player will be removed from the game and the club shall not be able to substitute another player on its roster.

(c) Each team shall be allowed one goalkeeper on the ice at one time. The goalkeeper may be removed and another player substituted. Such substitute shall not be permitted the privileges of the goalkeeper.

(d) Each team shall have on its bench, or on a chair immediately beside the bench, a substitute goalkeeper who shall, at all times, be fully dressed and equipped ready to play.

The substitute goalkeeper may enter the game at any time following a stoppage of play, but no warm-up shall be permitted.

(e) Except when both goalkeepers are incapacitated, no player in the playing roster in that game shall be permitted to wear the equipment of the goalkeeper.

(f) In regular League and playoff games, if both listed goalkeepers are incapacitated, that team shall be entitled to dress and play any available goalkeeper who is eligible. No delay shall be permitted in taking his position in the goal, and he shall be permitted a two-minute warm-up. However, the warm-up is not permitted in the event a goalkeeper is substituted for a penalty shot.

(g) The Referee shall report to the Commissioner for disciplinary action any delay in making a substitution of goalkeepers.

Rule 16. Starting Line-Up

(a) Prior to the start of the game, at the request of the Referee, the Manager or Coach of the visiting team is required to name the starting line-up to the Referee or Official Scorer. At any time in the game, at the request of the Referee made to the Captain, the visiting team must place a playing line-up on the ice and promptly commence play.

(b) Prior to the start of the game, the Manager or Coach of the home team, having been advised by the Official Scorer or the Referee the names of the starting line-up of the visiting team, shall name the starting line-up of the home team which information shall be conveyed by the Official Scorer or the Referee to the Coach of the visiting team.

(c) No change in the starting line-up of either team as given to the Referee or Official Scorer, or in the playing line-up on the ice, shall be made until the game is actually in progress. For an infraction of this rule, a bench minor penalty shall be imposed upon the offending team, provided such infraction is called to the attention of the Referee before the second face-off in the first period takes place.

Rule 17. Equalizing of Teams

DELETED

Rule 18. Change of Players

(a) Players may be changed at any time from the players' bench provided that the player or players leaving the ice shall be within five feet (5') of his players' bench and out of the play before the change is made.

A goalkeeper may be changed for another player at any time under the conditions set out in this section.

(NOTE 1) When a goalkeeper leaves his goal area and proceeds to his players' bench for the purpose of substituting another player, the rear Linesman shall be responsible to see

that the substitution made is not illegal by reason of the premature departure of the substitute from the bench (before the goalkeeper is within five feet (5') of the bench). If the substitution is made prematurely, the Linesman shall stop the play immediately by blowing his whistle unless the non-offending team has possession of the puck in which event the stoppage will be delayed until the puck changes hands. There shall be no time penalty to the team making the premature substitution but the resulting face-off will take place on the center "face-off spot".

(NOTE 2) The Referee shall request that the public address announcer make the following announcement: "Play has been stopped due to premature entry of a player from the players' bench." If in the course of making a substitution, the player entering the game plays the puck with his stick, skates or hands or who checks or makes any physical contact with an opposing player while the retiring player is actually on the ice, then the infraction of "too many men on the ice" will be called.

If in the course of a substitution either the player entering the play or the player retiring is struck by the puck accidentally, the play will not be stopped and no penalty will be called.

(b) If by reason of insufficient playing time remaining, or by reason of penalties already imposed, a bench minor penalty is imposed for deliberate illegal substitution (too many men on the ice) which cannot be served in its entirety within the legal playing time, a penalty shot shall be awarded against the offending team.

(c) A player serving a penalty on the penalty bench, who is to be changed after the penalty has been served, must proceed at once by way of the ice and be at his own players' bench before any change can be made.

For any violation of this rule, a bench minor penalty shall be imposed.

(d) Following the stoppage of play, the visiting team shall promptly place a lineup on the ice ready for play and no substitution shall be made from that time until play has been resumed. The home team may then make any desired substitution which does not result in the delay of the game.

If there is any undue delay by either team in changing lines, the Referee shall order the offending team or teams to take their positions immediately and not permit a line change.

(NOTE) When a substitution has been made under the above rule, no additional substitution may be made until play commences.

(e) The Referee shall give the visiting team a reasonable amount of time to make their change after which he shall put up his hand to indicate that no further change shall be made by the visiting club. At this point, the home team may change immediately. Any attempt by the visiting team to make a change after the Referee's signal shall result in the assessment of a bench minor penalty for delay of game.

Rule 19. Injured Players

(a) When a player other than a goalkeeper is injured or compelled to leave the ice during a game, he may retire from the game and be replaced by a substitute, but play must continue without the teams leaving the ice.

(b) If a goalkeeper sustains an injury or becomes ill, he must be ready to resume play immediately or be replaced by a substitute goalkeeper and NO additional time shall be allowed by the Referee for the purpose of enabling the injured or ill goalkeeper to resume his position. The substitute goalkeeper shall be allowed a two-minute warm-up during all pre-season games. No warm-up shall be permitted for a substitute goaltender in all regular season or playoff games. (See also Section (d).)

(c) The Referee shall report to the Commissioner for disciplinary action any delay in making a goalkeeper substitution.

The substitute goalkeeper shall be subject to the regular rules governing goalkeepers and shall be entitled to the same privileges.

(d) When a substitution for the regular goalkeeper has been made, such regular goalkeeper shall not resume his position until the first stoppage of play thereafter.

(e) If a penalized player has been injured, he may proceed to the dressing room without the necessity of taking a seat on the penalty bench. If the injured player receives a minor penalty, the penalized team shall immediately put a substitute player on the penalty bench, who shall serve the penalty without change. If the injured player receives a major penalty, the penalized team shall place a substitute player on the penalty bench before the penalty expires and no other replacement for the penalized player shall be permitted to enter the game except from the penalty bench. For violation of this rule, a bench minor penalty shall be imposed.

The penalized player who has been injured and been replaced on the penalty bench shall not be eligible to play until his penalty has expired.

(f) When a player is injured so that he cannot continue play or go to his bench, the play shall not be stopped until the injured player's team has secured possession of the puck; if the player's team is in possession of the puck at the time of injury, play shall be stopped immediately unless his team is in a scoring position.

(NOTE) In the case where it is obvious that a player has sustained a serious injury, the Referee and/or Linesman may stop the play immediately.

(g) When play has been stopped by the Referee or Linesman due to an injured player, such player must be substituted for immediately (except goalkeeper).

If when the attacking team has control of the puck in its attacking zone, play is stopped by reason of any injury to a player of the defending team, the face-off shall take place in the defending team's end zone face-off spot.

SECTION THREE – EQUIPMENT

(NOTE) A request for a measurement of any equipment covered by this section shall be limited to one request per team during the course of any stoppage in play.

Rule 20. Sticks

(a) The sticks shall be made of wood or other material approved by the Rules Committee, and must not have any projections. Adhesive tape of any colour may be wrapped around the stick at any place for the purpose of reinforcement or to improve control of the puck. In the case of a goalkeeper's stick, there shall be a knob of white tape or some other protective material approved by the League. This knob must not be less than one-half inch (½") thick at the top of the shaft.

Failure to comply with this provision of the Rule, the goalkeeper's stick is deemed unfit for play and must be changed without the application of a minor penalty.

(b) No stick shall exceed sixty inches (60') in length from the heel to the end of the shaft nor more than twelve and one-half inches (12½") from the heel to the end of the blade.

The blade of the stick shall not be more than three inches (3") in width at any point nor less than two inches (2"). All edges of the blade shall be beveled. The curvature of the blade of the stick shall be restricted in such a way that the distance of a perpendicular line measured from a straight line drawn from any point at the heel to the end of the blade to the point of maximum curvature shall not exceed one-half inch (½") .

(c) The blade of the goalkeeper's stick shall not exceed three and one-half inches (3½") in width at any point except at the heel where it must not exceed four and one-half inches (4½") in width; nor shall the goalkeeper's stick exceed fifteen and one-half inches (15½") in length from the heel to the end of the blade.

There is to be no measurement of the curvature of the blade on the goalkeeper's stick. All other elements of the stick are subject to a measurement and the appropriate applicable penalty.

The widened portion of the goalkeeper's stick extending up the shaft from the blade shall not extend more than twenty-six inches (26") from the heel and shall not exceed three and one-half inches (31⁄2") in width.

(d) A minor penalty plus a fine of two hundred dollars ($200) shall be imposed on any player or goalkeeper who uses a stick not conforming to the provisions of this rule.

(NOTE 1) When a formal complaint is made by the Captain or Alternate Captain of a team, against the dimensions of any stick, the Referee shall take the stick to the Timekeeper's bench where the necessary measurement shall be made immediately. The result shall be reported to the Penalty Timekeeper who shall record it on the back of the penalty record.

If the complaint is not sustained, a bench minor penalty shall be imposed against the complaining club in addition to a fine of one hundred dollars ($100).

(NOTE 2) A player who participates in the play while taking a replacement stick to his goalkeeper shall incur a minor penalty under this rule but the automatic fine of two hundred dollars ($200) shall not be imposed. If his participation causes a foul resulting in a penalty, the Referee shall report the incident to the Commissioner for disciplinary action.

NEW

(NOTE 3) A request for a stick measurement in overtime of any game is permitted, provided that such a request is not made following the scoring of a goal.

(e) In the event that a player scores on a penalty shot while using an illegal stick, the goal shall be disallowed and no further penalty imposed. However, if no goal is scored, the player taking the penalty shot shall receive a minor penalty.

(f) A minor penalty plus a ten-minute misconduct penalty shall be imposed on any player who refuses to surrender his stick for measurement when requested to do so by the Referee. In addition, this player shall be subject to a two hundred dollar ($200) fine.

Rule 21. Skates

(a) All hockey skates shall be of a design approved by the Rules Committee. All skates worn by players (but not goalkeepers) and by the Referee and Linesmen shall be equipped with an approved safety heel.

When the Referee becomes aware that any person is wearing a skate that does not have the approved safety heel, he shall direct its replacement at the next intermission. If such replacement is not carried out, the Referee shall report the incident to the Commissioner for disciplinary action.

(b) The use of speed skates or fancy skates or any skate so designed that it may cause injury is prohibited.

Rule 22. Goalkeeper's Equipment

(a) With the exception of skates and stick, all the equipment worn by the goalkeeper must be constructed solely for the purpose of protecting the head or body, and he must not wear any garment or use any contrivance which would give him undue assistance in keeping goal.

(NOTE) Cages on gloves and abdominal aprons extending down the front of the thighs on the outside of the pants are prohibited. "Cage" shall mean any lacing or webbing or other material in the goalkeeper's glove joining the thumb and index finger which is in excess of the minimum necessary to fill the gap when the goal-keeper's thumb and forefinger in the glove are fully extended and spread and includes any pocket or pouch effect produced by excess lacing or webbing or other material between the thumb and forefinger when fully extended or spread.

Protective padding attached to the back or forming part of goalkeeper's gloves shall not exceed eight inches (8") in width nor more than sixteen inches (16") in length at any point.

(b) The leg guards worn by goalkeepers shall not exceed twelve inches (12") in extreme width when on the leg of the player.

(NOTE) At the commencement of each season or at random during the season and prior to playoffs, goalkeepers' leg guards and gloves shall be checked by League staff and any violation of this rule shall be reported to the club involved and to the Commissioner of the League.

(c) Protective masks of a design approved by the Rules Committee may be worn by goalkeepers.

Rule 23. Protective Equipment

(a) All protective equipment, except gloves, headgear and goalkeepers' leg guards must be worn under the uniform. For violation of this rule, after warning by the Referee, a minor penalty shall be imposed.

(NOTE) Players including the goalkeeper violating this rule shall not be permitted to participate in game until such equipment has been corrected or removed.

(b) All players of both teams shall wear a helmet of design, material and construction approved by the Rules Committee at all times while participating in a game, either on the playing surface or the players' or penalty benches.

Players may elect for exemption from the operation of this sub-section (b) by execution of an approved Request and Release form and filing it with the League Office.

(c) A glove from which all or part of the palm has been removed or cut to permit the use of the bare hand shall be considered illegal equipment and if any player wears such a glove in play, a minor penalty shall be imposed on him.

When a complaint is made under this rule, and such complaint is not sustained, a bench minor penalty shall be imposed against the complaining club.

Rule 24. Dangerous Equipment

(a) The use of pads or protectors made of metal, or of any other material likely to cause injury to a player, is prohibited.

(NOTE) All elbow pads which do not have a soft protective outer covering of sponge rubber or similar material at least one-half inch (1/2") thick shall be considered dangerous equipment.

(b) A mask or protector of a design approved by the Rules Committee may be worn by a player who has sustained a facial injury.

In the first instance, the injured player shall be entitled to wear any protective device prescribed by the club doctor. If any opposing club objects to the device, it may record its objection with the Commissioner.

(NOTE) The Officiating Department is specifically authorized to make a check of each team's equipment to ensure the compliance with this rule. It shall report its findings to the Commissioner for his disciplinary action.

Rule 25. Puck

(a) The puck shall be made of vulcanized rubber, or other approved material, one inch (1") thick and three inches (3") in diameter and shall weigh between five and one-half ounces ($5\frac{1}{2}$ oz.) and six ounces (6 oz.). All pucks used in competition must be approved by the Rules Committee.

(b) The home team shall be responsible for providing an adequate supply of official pucks which shall be kept in a frozen condition. This supply of pucks shall be kept at the penalty bench under the control of one of the regular Off-ice Officials or a special attendant.

SECTION FOUR – PENALTIES

Rule 26. Penalties

Penalties shall be actual playing time and shall be divided in the following classes:

(1) Minor penalties

(2) Bench minor penalties

(3) Major penalties

(4) Misconduct penalties

(5) Match penalties

(6) Penalty shot

When coincident penalties are imposed on players of both teams, the penalized players of the visiting team shall take their positions on the penalty bench first in the place designated for visiting players.

(NOTE) When play is not actually in progress and an offense is committed by any player, the same penalty shall apply as though play was actually in progress.

Rule 27. Minor Penalties

(a) For a "MINOR PENALTY", any player, other than a goalkeeper, shall be ruled off the ice for two minutes during which time no substitute shall be permitted.

(b) A "BENCH MINOR" penalty involves the removal from the ice of one player of the team against which the penalty is assessed for a period of two minutes. Any player except a goalkeeper of the team may be designated to serve the penalty by the Manager or Coach through the playing Captain and such player shall take his place on the penalty bench promptly and serve the penalty as if it was a minor penalty imposed upon him.

(c) If while a team is "short-handed" by one or more minor or bench minor penalties, the opposing team scores a goal, the first of such penalties shall automatically terminate.

(NOTE) "Short-handed" means that the team must be below the numerical strength of its opponents on the ice at the time the goal is scored. The minor or bench minor penalty which terminates automatically is the one which causes the team scored against to be "short-handed". Thus coincident minor penalties to both teams do NOT cause either side to be "short-handed".

This rule shall also apply when a goal is scored on a penalty shot, or when an awarded goal is given.

When the minor penalties of two players of the same team terminate at the same time, the Captain of that team shall designate to the Referee which of such players will return to the ice first and the Referee will instruct the Penalty Timekeeper accordingly.

When a player receives a major penalty and a minor penalty at the same time, the major penalty shall be served first by the penalized player, except under Rule 28(c) in which case the minor penalty will be recorded and served first.

(NOTE) This applies to the case where BOTH penalties are imposed on the SAME player. See also Note to Rule 33.

(d) When ONE minor penalty is assessed to ONE player of EACH team at the same stoppage in play, these penalties will be served without substitution provided there are no other penalties in effect and visible on the penalty clocks.

Unless paragraph one of this Rule is applicable, when coincident minor penalties or coincident minor penalties of equal duration are imposed against players of both teams, the penalized players shall all take their places on the penalty benches and such penalized players shall not leave the penalty bench until the first stoppage of play following the expiry of their respective penalties. Immediate substitution shall be made for an equal number of minor penalties OR coincident minor penalties of equal duration to each team so penalized and the penalties of the players for which substitutions have been made shall not be taken into account for the purpose of the Delayed Penalty Rule (Rule 33).

Rule 28. Major Penalties

(a) For the first "MAJOR PENALTY" in any one game, the offender, except the goalkeeper, shall be ruled off the ice for five minutes during which time no substitute shall be permitted.

An automatic fine of one hundred dollars ($100) shall also be added when a major penalty is imposed for any foul causing injury to the face or head of an opponent by means of a stick.

(b) For the third major penalty in the same game to the same player, or for a major for butt-ending, cross-checking, high-sticking, slashing or spearing, he shall be ruled off the ice for the balance of the game, but a substitute shall be permitted to replace the player so suspended after five minutes have elapsed. (Major penalty plus game misconduct penalty with automatic fine of two hundred dollars ($200).)

(NOTE) In accordance with Rule 58(c) a goalkeeper shall not be assessed a game misconduct penalty when he is being assessed a major penalty for highsticking.

(c) When coincident major penalties or coincident penalties of equal duration, including a major penalty, are imposed against players of both teams, the penalized players shall all take their places on the penalty benches and such penalized players shall not leave the penalty benches until the first stoppage of play following the expiry of their respective penalties. Immediate substitutions shall be made for an equal number of major penalties, or coincident penalties of equal duration including a major penalty to each team so penalized, and the penalties of the players for which substitutions have been made shall not be taken into account for the purpose of the delayed penalty rule, (Rule 33).

Where it is required to determine which of the penalized players shall be designated to serve the delayed penalty under Rule 33 – Delayed Penalities, the penalized team shall have the right to make such designation not in conflict with Rule 27 – Minor Penalties.

Rule 29. Misconduct Penalties

MISCONDUCT
Place both hands on hips

(a) In the event of "MISCONDUCT" penalties to any players except the goalkeeper, the players shall be ruled off the ice for a period of ten minutes each. A substitute player is permitted to immediately replace a player serving a misconduct penalty. A player whose misconduct penalty has expired shall remain in the penalty box until the next stoppage of play.

When a player receives a minor penalty and a misconduct penalty at the same time, the penalized team shall immediately put a substitute player on the penalty bench and he shall serve the minor penalty without change.

When a player receives a major penalty and a misconduct penalty at the same time, the penalized team shall place a substitute player on the penalty bench before the major penalty expires and no replacement for the penalized player shall be permitted to enter the game except from the penalty bench. Any violation of this provision shall be treated as an illegal substitution under Rule 18 calling for a bench minor penalty.

(b) A misconduct penalty imposed on any player at any time shall be accompanied with an automatic fine of one hundred dollars ($100).

(c) A "GAME MISCONDUCT" penalty involves the suspension of a player for the balance of the game but a substitute is permitted to replace immediately the player so removed. A player incurring a game misconduct penalty shall incur an automatic fine of two hundred dollars ($200) and the case shall be reported to the Commissioner who shall have full power to impose such further penalties by way of suspension or fine on the penalized player or any other player involved in the altercation.

(d) The Referee may impose a "GROSS MISCONDUCT" penalty on any player, Manager, Coach or Trainer who is guilty of gross misconduct of any kind. Any person incurring a "gross misconduct" penalty shall be suspended for the balance of the game and shall incur an automatic fine of two hundred dollars ($200) and the case shall be referred to the Commissioner of the League for further disciplinary action.

(NOTE) For all game misconduct and gross misconduct penalties regardless of when imposed, a total of ten

minutes shall be charged in the records against the offending player.

(e) In regular League games, any player who incurs a total of three game misconduct penalties shall be suspended automatically for the next League game of his team. For each subsequent game misconduct penalty, the automatic suspension shall be increased by one game. For each suspension of a player, his club shall be fined one thousand dollars ($1000).

In playoff games, any player who incurs a total of two game misconduct penalties shall be suspended automatically for the next playoff game of his team. For each subsequent game misconduct penalty during the playoffs, the automatic suspension shall be increased by one game. For each suspension of a player during playoffs, his club shall be fined one thousand dollars ($1000).

(f) In regular League games, any player who incurs a total of two game misconduct penalties for stick related infractions penalized under Rule 28(b) shall be suspended automatically for the next League game of his team. For each subsequent game misconduct penalty, the automatic suspension shall be increased by one game.

In playoff games any player who incurs a total of two game misconduct penalties for stick related infractions penalized under Rule 28(b) shall be suspended automatically for the next playoff game of his team. For each subsequent game misconduct penalty during the playoffs the automatic suspension shall be increased by one game.

(NOTE) Any game misconduct penalty for which a player has been assessed an automatic suspension or supplementary discipline in the form of game suspension(s) by the Commissioner shall NOT be taken into account when calculating the total number of offenses under this subsection.

The automatic suspensions incurred under this subsection in respect to League games shall have no effect with respect to violations during playoff games.

Rule 30. Match Penalties

A "MATCH" penalty involves the suspension of a player for the balance of the game and the offender shall be ordered to the dressing room immediately. A substitute player is permitted to replace the penalized player after five minutes playing time has elapsed when the penalty is imposed under Rule 44 – Attempt to Injure or Rule 49 – Deliberate Injury of Opponents.

(NOTE 1) Regulations regarding additional penalties and substitutes are specifically covered in individual Rules 44, 49 and 64. Any additional penalty shall be served by a player to be designated by the Manager or Coach of the offending team through the playing Captain, such player to take his place in the penalty box immediately.

For all match penalties, regardless of when imposed, or prescribed additional penalties, a total of ten minutes shall be charged in the records against the offending player.

(NOTE 2) When coincident match penalties have been imposed under Rule 44, Rule 49 or Rule 64 to a player on both teams, Rule 28(c) covering coincident major penalties will be applicable with respect to player substitution.

(NOTE 3) The Referee is required to report all match penalties and the surrounding circumstances to the Commissioner of the League immediately following the game in which they occur.

Rule 31. Penalty Shot

(a) Any infraction of the rules which calls for a "PENALTY SHOT" shall be taken as follows:

The Referee shall ask to announce over the public address system the name of the player designated by him or selected by the team entitled to take the shot (as appropriate) and shall then place the puck on the center face-off spot and the player taking the shot will, on the instruction of the Referee, play the puck from there and shall attempt to score on the goalkeeper. The player taking the shot may carry the puck in any part of the neutral zone or his own defending zone but once the puck has crossed the attacking blue line it must be kept in motion towards the opponent's goal line and once it is shot, the play shall be considered complete. No goal can be scored on a rebound of any kind (an exception being the puck off the goal post, then the goalkeeper and then directly into the goal), and any time the puck crosses the goal line, the shot shall be considered complete.

Only a player designated as a goalkeeper or alternate goalkeeper may defend against the penalty shot.

(b) The goalkeeper must remain in his crease until the player taking the penalty shot has touched the puck and, in the event of violation of this rule or any foul committed by a goalkeeper, the Referee shall allow the shot to be taken and if the shot fails, he shall permit the penalty shot to be taken over again.

The goalkeeper may attempt to stop the shot in any manner except by throwing his stick or any object, in which case a goal shall be awarded.

(NOTE) See Rule 81.

(c) In cases where a penalty shot has been awarded under Rule 50(c), deliberately displacing goal post during course of a breakaway; under Rule 62(d), interference; under Rule 66(m), illegal entry into the game; under Rule 81(a) for throwing a stick; and under Rule 84(b), fouling from behind, the Referee shall designate the player who has been fouled as the player who shall take the penalty shot.

In cases where a penalty shot has been awarded under Rule 18(b), deliberate illegal substitution with insufficient playing time remaining; under Rule 50(d), deliberately displacing goal post; under Rule 53(c), falling on the puck in the crease; under Rule 57(d), picking up the puck from the crease area, the penalty shot shall be taken by a player selected by the Captain of the non-offending team from the players on the ice at the time when the foul was committed. Such selection shall be reported to the Referee and cannot be changed.

If by reason of injury, the player designated by the Referee to take the penalty shot is unable to do so within a reasonable time, the shot may be taken by a player selected by the Captain of the non-offending team from the players on the ice when the foul was committed. Such selection shall be reported to the Referee and cannot be changed.

(d) Should the player in respect to whom a penalty shot has been awarded himself commit a foul in connection with the same play or circumstances, either before or after the penalty shot has been awarded, be designated to take the shot, he shall first be permitted to do so before being sent to the penalty bench to serve the penalty except when such penalty is for a game misconduct, gross misconduct or match penalty in which case the penalty shot shall be taken by a player selected by the Captain of the non-offending team from the players on the ice at the time when the foul was committed.

If at the time a penalty shot is awarded, the goalkeeper of the penalized team has been removed from the ice to substitute another player, the goalkeeper shall be permitted to return to the ice before the penalty shot is taken.

(e) While the penalty shot is being taken, players of both sides shall withdraw to the sides of the rink and in front of their own player's bench.

(f) If, while the penalty shot is being taken, any player of the opposing team shall have by some action interfered with or distracted the player taking the shot and, because of such action, the shot should have failed, a second attempt shall be permitted and the Referee shall impose a misconduct penalty on the player so interfering or distracting.

(g) If a goal is scored from a penalty shot, the puck shall be faced-off at center ice. If a goal is not scored, the puck shall be faced-off at either of the end face-off spots in the zone in which the penalty shot was tried.

(h) Should a goal be scored from a penalty shot, a further penalty to the offending player shall not be applied unless the offense for which the penalty shot was awarded was such as to incur a major or match penalty or misconduct penalty, in which case the penalty prescribed for the particular offense shall be imposed.

If the offense for which the penalty shot was awarded was such as would normally incur a minor penalty, then regardless of whether the penalty shot results in a goal or not, no further minor penalty shall be served.

(i) If the foul upon which the penalty shot is based occurs during actual playing time, the penalty shot shall be awarded and taken immediately in the usual manner notwithstanding any delay occasioned by a slow whistle by the Referee to permit the play to be completed, which delay results in the expiry of the regular playing time in any period.

The time required for the taking of a penalty shot shall not be included in the regular playing time or overtime.

Rule 32. Goalkeeper's Penalties

(a) A goalkeeper shall not be sent to the penalty bench for an offense which incurs a minor penalty, but instead, the minor penalty shall be served by another member of his team who was on the ice when the offense was committed, said player to be designated by the Manager or

Coach of the offending team through the playing Captain and such substitute shall not be changed.

(NOTE) A penalized player may not serve a goalkeeper's penalty.

(b) A goalkeeper shall not be sent to the penalty bench for an offense which incurs a major penalty, but instead, the major penalty shall be served by another member of his team who was on the ice when the offense was committed, said player to be designated by the Manager or Coach of the offending team through the playing Captain and such substitute shall not be changed.

(c) Should a goalkeeper incur three major penalties in one game penalized under Rule 28(b) – Major Penalties, he shall be ruled off the ice for the balance of the playing time and his place shall be taken by a member of his own club, or by a regular substitute goalkeeper who is available. Such player will be allowed the goalkeeper's equipment. (Major penalty plus game misconduct penalty and automatic fine of two hundred dollars ($200).)

(d) Should a goalkeeper on the ice incur a misconduct penalty, this penalty shall be served by another member of his team who was on the ice when the offense was committed, said player to be designated by the Manager or Coach of the offending team through the Captain and, in addition, the goalkeeper shall be fined one hundred dollars ($100).

(e) Should a goalkeeper incur a game misconduct penalty, his place will then be taken by a member of his own club, or by a regular substitute goalkeeper who is available, and such player will be allowed the goalkeeper's full equipment. In addition, the goalkeeper shall be fined two hundred dollars ($200).

(f) Should a goalkeeper incur a match penalty, his place will then be taken by a member of his own club, or by a substitute goalkeeper who is available, and such player will be allowed the goalkeeper's full equipment. However, any additional penalties as specifically called for by the individual rules covering match penalties will apply, and the offending team shall be penalized accordingly, such additional penalties to be served by other members of the team on the ice when the offenses were committed, said players to be designated by the Manager or Coach of the offending team through the Captain. (See Rules 44, 49 and 64.)

(g) Should a goalkeeper incur a match penalty, the case shall be investigated promptly by the Commissioner who shall have full power to fine or suspend the penalized goalkeeper or any other players in the altercation.

(h) A minor penalty shall be imposed on a goalkeeper who leaves the immediate vicinity of his crease during an altercation. In addition, he shall be subject to a fine of two hundred dollars ($200) and this incident shall be reported to the Commissioner for such further disciplinary action as may be required.

(NOTE) All penalties imposed on a goalkeeper, regardless of who serves the penalty or any substitution, shall be charged in the records against the goalkeeper.

(i) If a goalkeeper participates in the play in any manner when he is beyond the center red line, a minor penalty shall be imposed upon him.

Rule 33. Delayed Penalties

(a) If a third player of any team shall be penalized while two players of the same team are serving penalties, the penalty time of the third player shall not commence until the penalty time of one of the two players already penalized has

DELAYED CALLING OF PENALTY
Referee extends arm and points to penalized player.

elapsed. Nevertheless, the third player penalized must at once proceed to the penalty bench but may be replaced by a substitute until such time as the penalty time of the penalized player shall commence.

(b) When any team shall have three players serving penalties at the same time and because of the delayed penalty rule, a substitute for the third offender is on the ice, none of the three penalized players on the penalty bench may return to the ice until play has stopped. When play has been stopped, the player whose full penalty has expired may return to the play.

Provided however that the Penalty Timekeeper shall permit the return to the ice in the order of expiry of their penalties, of a player or players when, by reason of the expiration of their penalties, the penalized team is entitled to have more than four players on the ice.

(c) In the case of delayed penalties, the Referee shall instruct the Penalty Timekeeper that penalized players whose penalties have expired shall only be allowed to return to the ice when there is a stoppage of play.

When the penalties of two players of the same team will expire at the same time, the Captain of that team will designate to the Referee which of such players will return to the ice first and the Referee will instruct the Penalty Timekeeper accordingly.

When a major and a minor penalty are imposed at the same time on players of the same team, the Penalty Timekeeper shall record the minor as being the first of such penalties.

(NOTE) This applies to the case where the two penalties are imposed on DIFFERENT players of the same team. See also Note to Rule 27.

Rule 34. Calling of Penalties

(a) Should an infraction of the rules which would call for a minor, major, misconduct, game misconduct or match penalty be committed by a player of the side in possession of the puck, the Referee shall immediately blow his whistle and penalize the offending player.

The resulting face-off shall be made at the place where the play was stopped unless the stoppage occurs in the attacking zone of the player penalized in which case the face-off shall be made at the nearest face-off spot in the neutral zone.

(b) Should an infraction of the rules which would call for a minor, major, misconduct, game misconduct or match penalty be committed by a player of the team not in possession of the puck, the Referee will blow his whistle and impose the penalty on the offending player upon completion of the play by the team in possession of the puck.

(NOTE) There shall be no signal given by the Referee for a misconduct or game misconduct penalty under this section.

The resulting face-off shall be made at the place where the play was stopped, unless during the period of a delayed whistle due to a foul by a player of the side NOT in possession, the side in possession ices the puck, shoots the puck so that it goes out of bounds or is unplayable, then the face-off following the stoppage shall take place in the neutral zone near the defending blue line of the team shooting the puck.

If the penalty to be imposed is a minor penalty and a goal is scored on the play by the non-offending side, the minor penalty shall not be imposed but major and match penalties shall be imposed in the normal manner regardless of whether or not a goal is scored.

When the penalty to be imposed is applicable under Rule 58(c)(1) – High Sticks or Rule 79 (c) – Spearing and Butt-Ending, and a goal is scored, two minutes of the appropriate penalty will be assessed to the offending player. (This will be announced as a double minor for the appropriate foul and the player will serve two minutes only.)

(NOTE 1) "Completion of the play by the team in possession" in this rule means that the puck must have come into the possession and control of an opposing player or has been "frozen". This does not mean a rebound off the goalkeeper, the goal or the boards, or any accidental contact with the body or equipment of an opposing player.

(NOTE 2) If after the Referee has signalled a penalty but before the whistle has been blown, the puck shall enter the goal of the non-offending team as the direct result of a player of that team, the goal shall be allowed and the penalty signalled shall be imposed in the normal manner.

(NOTE 3) If when a team is "short-handed" by reason of one or more minor or bench minor penalties, the Referee signals a further minor

penalty or penalties against the "short-handed" team and a goal is scored by the non-offending side before the whistle is blown, then the goal shall be allowed. The penalty or penalties signalled shall be assessed and the first of the minor penalties already being served shall automatically terminate under Rule 27(c) – Minor Penalties.

(c) Should the same offending player commit other fouls on the same play, either before or after the Referee has blown his whistle, the offending player shall serve such penalties consecutively.

Rule 34A. Supplementary Discipline

In addition to the automatic fines and suspensions imposed under these rules, the Commissioner may, at his discretion, investigate any incident that occurs in connection with any exhibition, League or playoff game and may assess additional fines and/or suspensions for any offense committed during the course of a game or any aftermath thereof by a player, Trainer, Manager, Coach or club executive, whether or not such offense has been penalized by the Referee.

(NOTE) If an investigation is requested by a club or by the League on its own initiative, it must be initiated within seventy-two (72) hours following the completion of the game in which the incident occurred.

Rule 34B. Suspensions Arising from Exhibition Games

Whenever suspensions are imposed as a result of infractions occurring during exhibition games, the Commissioner shall exercise his discretion in scheduling the suspensions to ensure that no team shall be short more players in any regular League game than it would have been had the infractions occurred in regular League games.

SECTION FIVE – OFFICIALS

Rule 35. Appointment of Officials

(a) The Commissioner shall appoint a Referee, two Linesmen, Game Timekeeper, Penalty Timekeeper, Official Scorer and two Goal Judges for each game.

(b) The Commissioner shall forward to all clubs a list of Referees, Linesmen, and Off-ice Officials, all of whom must be treated with proper respect at all times during the season by all players and officials of clubs.

Rule 36. Referee

(a) The REFEREE shall have general supervision of the game and shall have full control of all game officials and players during the game, including stoppages; and in case of any dispute, his decision shall be final. The Referee shall remain on the ice at the conclusion of each period until all players have proceeded to their dressing rooms.

(b) All Referees and Linesmen shall be dressed in black trousers and official sweaters.

They shall be equipped with approved whistles and metal tape measures with minimum length of six feet.

(c) The Referee shall order the teams on the ice at the appointed time for the beginning of a game and at the commencement of each period. If for any reason, there is more than fifteen minutes' delay in the commencement of the game or any undue delay in resuming play after the fifteen-minute intervals between periods, the Referee shall state in his report to the Commissioner the cause of the delay and the club or clubs which were at fault.

(d) It shall be his duty to see to it that all players are properly dressed, and that the approved regulation equipment is in use at all times during the game.

(e) The Referee shall, before starting the game, see that the appointed Game Timekeeper, Penalty Timekeeper, Official Scorer and Goal Judges are in their respective places and satisfy himself that the timing and signalling equipment are in order.

(f) It shall be his duty to impose such penalties as are prescribed by the rules for infractions thereof and he shall give the final decision in matters of disputed goals. The Referee may consult with the

Linesmen, Goal Judge or Video Goal Judge before making his decision.

(g) The Referee shall announce to the Official Scorer or Penalty Timekeeper all goals legally scored as well as penalties, and for what infractions such penalties are imposed.

The Referee shall cause to be announced over the public address system the reason for not allowing a goal every time the goal signal light is turned on in the course of play. This shall be done at the first stoppage of play regardless of any standard signal given by the Referee when the goal signal light was put on in error.

The Referee shall report to the Official Scorer the name or number of the goal scorer but he shall not give any information or advice with respect to assist.

(NOTE) The name of the scorer and any player entitled to an assist will be announced on the public address system. In the event that the Referee disallows a goal for any violation of the rules, he shall report the reason for disallowance to the Official Scorer who shall announce the Referee's decision correctly over the public address system.

The infraction of the rules for which each penalty has been imposed will be announced correctly, as reported by the Referee, over the public address system. Where players of both teams are penalized on the same play, the penalty to the visiting player will be announced first.

Where a penalty is imposed by the Referee which calls for a mandatory or automatic fine, only the time portion of the penalty will be reported by the Referee to the Official Scorer and announced on the public address system, and the fine will be collected through the League office.

(h) The Referee shall see to it that players of opposing teams are separated on the penalty bench to prevent feuding.

(i) He shall not halt the game for any infractions of the rules concerning off-side play at the blue line or center line, or any violation of Rule 61, icing the puck. Determining infractions of these rules is the duty of the Linesmen unless, by virtue of some accident, the Linesman is prevented from doing so in which case the duties of the Linesman shall be assumed by the Referee until play is stopped.

(j) Should a Referee accidentally leave the ice or receive an injury which incapacitates him from discharging his duties while play is in progress, the game shall be automatically stopped.

(k) If, through misadventure or sickness, the Referee and Linesmen appointed are prevented from appearing, the Managers or Coaches of the two clubs shall agree on a Referee and Linesman. If they are unable to agree, they shall appoint a player from each side who shall act as Referee and Linesman; the player of the home club acting as Referee and the player of the visiting club as Linesman.

(l) If the regularly appointed officials appear during the progress of the game, they shall at once replace the temporary officials.

(m) Should a Linesman appointed be unable to act at the last minute or through sickness or accident be unable to finish the game, the Referee shall have the power to appoint another in his stead, if he deems it necessary, or if required to do so by the Manager or Coach of either of the competing teams.

(n) If, owing to illness or accident, the Referee is unable to continue to officiate, one of the Linesmen shall perform the duties of the Referee during the balance of the game, the Linesman to be selected by the Referee. In the event that an NHL Supervisor is in attendance at a game where a spare official is present, he shall have the authority to substitute the injured Referee with the spare official.

(o) The Referee shall check club rosters and all players in uniform before signing reports of the game.

(p) The Referee shall report to Commissioner promptly and in detail the circumstances of any of the following incidents:

(i) When a stick or part thereof is thrown outside the playing area – Rule 81(c) – Throwing Stick;

(ii) Every obscene gesture made by any person involved in the playing or conduct of the game whether as a participant or as an official of either team or of the League, which gesture he has personally observed or which has been brought to his attention by any game official – Rule 68(a) – Obscene or Profane Language or Gestures;

(iii) When any player, Trainer, Coach or club executive becomes involved in an altercation with a spectator – Rule 63(b) – Interference by/with Spectators;

(iv) Every infraction under Rule 28(b) – Major Penalties, major and game misconducts.

(q) In the event of failure by a club to comply with a provision of the League constitution, by-laws, resolutions, rules or regulations affecting the playing of a game, the Referee shall, if so directed by the Commissioner or his designee, refuse to permit the game to proceed until the offending club comes into compliance with such provision.

Should the offending club persist in its refusal to come into compliance, the Referee shall, with the prior approval of the Commissioner or his designee, declare the game forfeited and the non-offending club the winner. Should the Referee declare the game forfeited because both clubs have refused to comply with such a provision, the visiting club shall be declared the winner.

If the game is declared forfeited prior to its having commenced, the score shall be recorded as 1-0 and no player shall be credited with any personal statistics.

If the game was in progress at the time it is declared forfeited, the score shall be recorded as zero for the loser and 1, or such greater number of goals that had been scored by it, for the winner;

however, the players on both clubs shall be credited with all personal statistics earned up to the time the forfeit was declared.

Rule 37. Linesman

(a) The duty of the LINESMAN is to determine any infractions of the rules concerning off-side play at the blue line or center line, or any violation of Rule 61, icing the puck.

He shall stop the play when the puck goes outside the playing area, when it is interfered with by any ineligible person, when it is struck above the height of the shoulder and when the goal post has been displaced from its normal position. He shall stop the play for off-sides occurring on face-offs and for premature entry into face-off circles. He shall stop the play when he has observed that a goal has been scored which has not been observed by the Referee. He shall stop the play when there has been a premature substitution for a goalkeeper under Rule 18(a) – Change of Players; for injured players under Rule 19(f) – Injured Players; for a player batting the puck forward to a teammate under Rule 57(e) – Handling Puck with Hands; the calling of a double-minor penalty for accidental high sticks, under Rule 58(c) – High Sticks; interference by spectators under Rule 63(a) – Interference by/with spectators; the calling of a double-minor penalty to a player who attempts to poke, jab, spear or butt-end an opponent, under Rule 79(c) – Spearing and Butt-ending; and the calling of a penalty under Rule 81(a) – Throwing Stick, for deliberately throwing a stick in the defensive zone.

(b) He shall face-off the puck at all times, except at the start of the game, at the beginning of each period and after a goal has been scored.

The Referee may call upon a Linesman to conduct a face-off at any time.

(c) He shall, when requested to do so by the Referee, give his version of any incident that may have taken place during the playing of the game.

(d) He shall not stop the play to impose any penalty except when a major penalty is warranted to a player on the ice when a serious incident has been observed by him but not by the Referee and/or when he observes any violation of Rules 18(a) and (c), change of players (too many men on the ice); Rule 42(k), articles thrown on the ice from vicinity of players' or penalty bench; Rule 42(l), interference with game officials by player, Coach,

Trainer or club executive; Rule 46(c), stick thrown on ice from players' bench and Rule 50(c), delaying the game by deliberately displacing the post from its normal position. He shall report such violation to the Referee who shall impose a bench minor penalty against the offending team.

In addition, when assessing a major penalty to a player, he may, at his discretion, assess a minor penalty to a player of the opposing team that he deems instigated the incident for which the major penalty was assessed.

He shall report immediately to the Referee his version of the circumstances with regard to interference on a goaltender when a goal is scored.

He shall report immediately to the Referee his version of any infraction of the rules constituting a major or match foul or game misconduct or any conduct calling for a bench minor penalty or misconduct penalty under these rules.

Rule 38. Goal Judge

(a) There shall be one GOAL JUDGE at each goal. They shall not be members of either club engaged in a game, nor shall they be replaced during its progress, unless after the commencement of the game it becomes apparent that either Goal Judge, on account of partisanship or any other cause, is guilty of giving unjust decisions, when the Referee may appoint another Goal Judge to act in his stead.

(b) Goal Judges shall be stationed behind the goals during the progress of play, in properly protected areas, if possible, so that there can be no interference with their activities. They shall not change goals during the game.

(c) In the event of a goal being claimed, the Goal Judge of that goal shall decide whether or not the puck has passed between the goal posts and entirely over the goal line.

Rule 39. Penalty Timekeeper

(a) The PENALTY TIMEKEEPER shall keep, on the official forms provided, a correct record of all penalties imposed by the officials including the names of the players penalized, the infractions penalized, the duration of each penalty and the time at which each penalty was imposed. He shall report in the Penalty Record each penalty shot awarded, the name of the player taking the shot and the result of the shot.

(b) The Penalty Timekeeper shall check and ensure that the time served by all penalized players is correct. He shall be responsible for the correct posting of penalties on the scoreboard at all times and shall promptly call to the attention of the Referee any discrepancy between the time recorded on the clock and the official correct time and he shall be responsible for making any adjustments ordered by the Referee.

He shall upon request, give a penalized player correct information as to the unexpired time of his penalty.

(NOTE 1) The infraction of the rules for which each penalty has been imposed will be announced twice over the public address system as reported by the Referee. Where players of both teams are penalized on the same play, the penalty to the visiting player will be announced first.

(NOTE 2) Misconduct penalties and coincident major penalties should not be recorded on the timing device but such penalized players should be alerted and released at the first stoppage of play following the expiration of their penalties.

(c) Upon the completion of each game, the Penalty Timekeeper shall complete and sign four copies of the Penalty Record to be distributed as quickly as possible to the following persons:

(1) One copy to the Official Scorer for transmission to the League Commissioner;

(2) One copy to the visiting Coach or Manager;

(3) One copy to the home Coach or Manager;

(4) One copy to the home team Public Relations Department.

(d) The Officiating Department shall be entitled to inspect, collect and forward to League headquarters the actual work sheets used by the Penalty Timekeeper in any game.

Rule 40. Official Scorer

(a) Before the start of the game, the Official Scorer shall obtain from the Manager or Coach of both teams a list of all eligible players and the starting line-up of each team which information shall be made known to the opposing Manager or Coach before the start of play, either personally or through the Referee.

The Official Scorer shall secure the names of the Captain and Alternate Captains from the Manager or Coach at the time the line-ups are collected and will indicate those nominated by placing the letter "C" or "A" opposite their names on the Referee's Report of Match. All this information shall be presented to the Referee for his signature at the completion of the game.

(b) The Official Scorer shall keep a record of the goals scored, the scorers, and players to whom assists have been credited and shall indicate those players on the lists who have actually taken part in the game. He shall also record the time of entry into the game of any substitute goalkeeper. He shall record on the Official Score Sheet a notation where a goal is scored when the goalkeeper has been removed from the ice.

(c) The Official Scorer shall award the points for goals and assists and his decision shall be final. The awards of points for goals and assists shall be announced twice over the public address system and all changes in such awards shall also be announced in the same manner.

No requests for changes in any award of points shall be considered unless they are made at or before the conclusion of actual play in the game by the team Captain.

(d) At the conclusion of the game, the Official Scorer shall complete and sign four copies of the Official Score Sheet for distribution as quickly as possible to the following persons:

(1) One copy to the Official Scorer to be transmitted to the League Commissioner;

(2) One copy to the visiting Coach or Manager;

(3) One copy to the home Coach or Manager;

(4) One copy to the home team Public Relations Department.

(e) The Official Scorer shall also prepare the Official Report of Match for signature by the Referee and forward it to the League Commissioner together with the Official Score Sheet and the Penalty Record.

(f) The Official Scorer should be in an elevated position, well away from the players' benches, with house telephone communication to the public address announcer.

Rule 41. Game Timekeeper

(a) The Game Timekeeper shall record the time of starting and finishing of each period in the game. During the game the game timekeeper will start the clock with the drop of the puck and stop the clock upon hearing the Official's whistle or the scoring of a goal.

(b) The Game Timekeeper shall signal the Referee and the competing teams for the start of the game and each succeeding period and the Referee shall start the play promptly in accordance with Rule 82 – Time of Match.

For the purpose of keeping the spectators informed as to the time remaining during intermissions, the Game Timekeeper will use the electric clock to record the length of intermissions. The clock will not start for the intermission until all players and officials have left the ice.

To assist in assuring the prompt return to the ice of the teams and the officials, the Game Timekeeper shall give preliminary warnings five and two minutes prior to the resumption of play in each period.

(c) If the rink is not equipped with an automatic signalling device or, if such device fails to function, the Game Timekeeper shall signal the end of each period by blowing a whistle.

(d) He shall cause to be announced on the public address system at the nineteenth minute in each period that there is one minute remaining to be played in the period.

(e) In the event of any dispute regarding time, the matter shall be referred to the Referee for adjustment and his decision shall be final.

(f) The Game Timekeeper is required to synchronize his timing device with the Television Producer of the originating broadcast.

Rule 41A. Statistician

(a) There shall be appointed for duty at every game played in the League a Statistician and such assistants or alternates as may be deemed necessary.

(b) The duty of the Statistician(s) is to correctly record on official League forms all of the required data concerning the performances of the individual players and teams.

(c) These records shall be compiled and recorded in strict conformity with the instructions printed on the forms supplied and shall be completed as to totals where required and with such accuracy as to ensure that the data supplied is "in balance".

(d) At the conclusion of each game, the Statistician shall sign and distribute four copies of the final and correct Statistician's Report to each of the following persons:

   (1) One copy to the Official Scorer for transmission to the League Commissioner;

   (2) One copy to the visiting Coach or Manager;

   (3) One copy to the home Coach or Manager;

   (4) One copy to the home team Public Relations Department.

SECTION SIX – PLAYING RULES

Rule 42. Abuse of Officials and other Misconduct

(NOTE) In the enforcement of this rule, the Referee has, in many instances, the option of imposing a misconduct penalty or a bench minor penalty. In principle, the Referee is directed to impose a bench minor penalty in respect to the violations which occur on or in the immediate vicinity of the players' bench but off the playing surface and in all cases affecting non-playing personnel or players. A misconduct penalty should be imposed for violations which occur on the playing surface or in the penalty bench area and where the penalized player is readily identifiable.

(a) A misconduct penalty shall be imposed on any player who uses obscene, profane or abusive language to any person or who intentionally knocks or shoots the puck out of the reach of an official who is retrieving it or who deliberately throws any equipment out of the playing area.

UNSPORTSMANLIKE CONDUCT
Use both hands to form a "T" in front of the chest.

(b) A minor penalty shall be assessed to any player who challenges or disputes the rulings of any official during a game. If the player persists in such challenge or dispute, he shall be assessed a misconduct penalty and any further dispute will result in a game misconduct penalty being assessed to the offending player.

In the event that a teammate of a penalized player challenges or disputes the ruling of the official in assessing the penalty, a misconduct penalty shall be imposed.

NEW

(NOTE:) Any player who, having entered the penalty bench, leaves the penalty bench prior to the expiration of his penalty, shall be assessed the appropriate penalties. He shall also be automatically suspended for the next three Regular League and/or Playoff games of his club. This rule does not replace any other more severe penalty that may be imposed for leaving the penalty bench. See also Rule 66 – Leaving Players' or Penalty Bench.

(c) A misconduct penalty shall be imposed on any player or players who bang the boards with their sticks or other objects at any time, showing disrespect for an Official's decision.

In the event that the Coach, Trainer, Manager or club executive commits an infraction under this rule, a bench minor penalty shall be imposed.

(d) Where coincident penalties are imposed on players of both teams, the penalized players of the visiting team shall take their positions on the penalty bench first in the place designated for visiting players.

(e) Any player who, following a fight or other altercation in which he has been involved is broken up and for which he is penalized, fails to proceed directly and immediately to the penalty bench, or who causes any delay by retrieving his equipment (gloves, sticks, etc. shall be delivered to him at the penalty bench by teammates), shall incur an automatic fine of one hundred dollars ($100) in addition to all other penalties or fines incurred.

(f) Any player who persists in continuing or attempting to continue a fight or altercation after he has been ordered by the Referee to stop, or who resists a Linesman in the discharge of his duties shall, at the discretion of the Referee, incur a misconduct or game misconduct penalty in addition to any penalties imposed.

(g) A misconduct penalty shall be imposed on any player who, after warning by the Referee, persists in any course of conduct (including threatening or abusive language or gestures or similar actions) designed to incite an opponent into incurring a penalty.

If, after the assessment of a misconduct penalty, a player persists in any course of conduct for which he was previously assessed a misconduct penalty, he shall be assessed a game misconduct penalty.

(h) A bench minor penalty shall be imposed against the offending team if any player, club executive, Manager, Coach or

Trainer uses obscene, profane or abusive language or gesture to any person or uses the name of any official coupled with any vociferous remarks.

(i) In the case of any club executive, Manager, Coach or Trainer being guilty of such misconduct, he is to be removed from the bench by order of the Referee and his case reported to the Commissioner for further action.

(j) If any club executive, Manager, Coach or Trainer is removed from the bench by order of the Referee, he must not sit near the bench of his club nor in any way direct or attempt to direct the play of his club.

When a Coach has been removed from the bench, he shall be assessed a Game Misconduct penalty.

(k) A bench minor penalty shall be imposed against the offending team if any player, Trainer, Coach, Manager or club executive in the vicinity of the players' bench or penalty bench throws anything on the ice during the progress of the game or during stoppage of play.

(NOTE) The penalty provided under this rule is in addition to any penalty imposed under Rule 46(c) – Broken Stick.

(l) A bench minor penalty shall be imposed against the offending team if any player, Trainer, Coach, Manager or club executive interferes in any manner with any game official including Referee, Linesmen, Timekeepers or Goal Judges in the performance of their duties.

The Referee may assess further penalties under Rule 67 (Abuse of Officials) if he deems them to be warranted.

(m) A misconduct penalty shall be imposed on any player or players who, except for the purpose of taking their positions on the penalty bench, enter or remain in the Referee's crease while he is reporting to or consulting with any game official including Linesmen, Timekeeper, Penalty Timekeeper, Official Scorer or Announcer.

(n) A minor penalty shall be imposed on any player who is guilty of unsportsmanlike conduct including, but not limited to hair-pulling, biting, grabbing hold of face mask, etc.

(NOTE) If warranted the Referee may apply Rule 29(d) – Gross Misconduct.

(o) A minor penalty shall be imposed on a player who attempts to draw a penalty by his actions ("diving").

Rule 43. Adjustment to Clothing or Equipment

(a) Play shall not be stopped nor the game delayed by reasons of adjustments to clothing, equipment, skates or sticks.

For an infringement of this rule, a minor penalty shall be given.

(b) The onus of maintaining clothing and equipment in proper condition shall be upon the player. If adjustments are required, the player shall leave the ice and play shall continue with a substitute.

(c) No delay shall be permitted for the repair or adjustment of goalkeeper's equipment. If adjustments are required, the goalkeeper shall leave the ice and his place shall be taken by the substitute goalkeeper immediately.

(d) For an infraction of this rule by a goalkeeper, a minor penalty shall be imposed.

Rule 44. Attempt to Injure

(a) A match penalty shall be imposed on any player who deliberately attempts to injure an opponent and the circumstances shall be reported to the Commissioner for further action. A substitute for the penalized player shall be permitted at the end of the fifth minute.

(b) A game misconduct penalty shall be imposed on any player who deliberately attempts to injure an Official, Manager, Coach or Trainer in any manner and the circumstances shall be reported to the Commissioner for further action.

(NOTE) The Commissioner, upon preliminary investigation indicating the probable imposition of supplementary disciplinary action, may order the immediate suspension of a player who has incurred a match penalty under this rule, pending the final determination of such supplementary disciplinary action.

Rule 45. Board Checking and Checking from Behind

(a) A minor or major penalty, at the discretion of the Referee based upon the degree of violence of the impact with the boards, shall be imposed on any player who bodychecks, cross-checks, elbows, charges or trips an opponent in such a manner that causes the opponent to be thrown violently into the boards.

BOARDING
Pounding the closed fist of one hand into the open palm of the other hand.

(NOTE) Any unnecessary contact with a player playing the puck on an obvious "icing" or "off-side" play which results in that player being knocked into the boards is "boarding" and must be penalized as such. In other instances where there is no contact with the boards, it should be treated as "charging".

"Rolling" an opponent (if he is the puck carrier) along the boards where he is endeavoring to go through too small an opening is not boarding. However, if the opponent is not the puck carrier, then such action should be penalized as boarding, charging, interference or, if the arms or stick are employed, it should be called holding or hooking.

(b) When a major penalty is imposed under this rule, an automatic fine of one hundred dollars ($100) shall be imposed.

(c) When a major penalty is imposed under this rule for a foul resulting in an injury to the face or head of an opponent, an automatic game misconduct shall be imposed.

NEW

(d) Any player who cross-checks, pushes or charges from behind an opponent who is unable to defend himself, shall be assessed a major and a game misconduct. This penalty applies anywhere on the playing surface.

(e) In regular season games any player who incurs a total of two game misconduct penalties for board-checking under Rule 45(c) and (d) shall be suspended automatically for the next League game of his team. For each subsequent game misconduct penalty the automatic suspension shall be increased by one game.

In playoff games, any player who incurs a total of two game misconduct penalties for board-checking under Rule 45(c) and (d) shall be suspended automatically for the next playoff game of his team. For each subsequent game misconduct penalty during the playoffs the automatic suspension shall be increased by one game.

Rule 46. Broken Stick

(a) A player without a stick may participate in the game. A player whose stick is broken may participate in the game provided he drops the broken portion. A minor penalty shall be imposed for an infraction of this rule.

(NOTE) A broken stick is one which, in the opinion of the Referee, is unfit for normal play.

(b) A goalkeeper may continue to play with a

broken stick until stoppage of play or until he has been legally provided with a stick.

(c) A player whose stick is broken may not receive a stick thrown on the ice from any part of the rink but must obtain same at his players' bench. A goalkeeper whose stick is broken may not receive a stick thrown on the ice from any part of the rink but may receive a stick from a teammate without proceeding to his players' bench. A minor penalty shall be imposed on the player or goalkeeper receiving a stick illegally under this rule.

(d) A goalkeeper whose stick is broken or illegal may not go to the players' bench for a replacement but must receive his stick from a teammate.

For an infraction of this rule, a minor penalty shall be imposed on the goalkeeper.

Rule 47. Charging

(a) A minor or major penalty shall be imposed on a player who runs or jumps into or charges an opponent.

(b) When a major penalty is imposed under this rule for a foul resulting in injury to the face or head of an opponent, an automatic fine of one hundred dollars

CHARGING
Rotating clenched fists around one another in front of chest.

($100) shall be imposed.

(c) A minor or major penalty shall be imposed on a player who charges a goalkeeper while the goalkeeper is within his goal crease.

(NOTE) If more than two steps or strides are taken, it shall be considered a charge.

A goalkeeper is NOT "fair game" just because he is outside the goal crease area. A penalty for interference or charging (minor or major) should be called in every case where an opposing player makes unnecessary contact with a goalkeeper.

Likewise, Referees should be alert to penalize goalkeepers for tripping, slash-ing or spearing in the vicinity of the goal.

Rule 48. Cross-Checking

(a) A minor or major penalty, at the discretion of the Referee, shall be imposed on a player who "cross-checks" an opponent.

(NOTE 1) Cross-check shall mean a check delivered with both hands on the stick and no part of the stick on the ice.

CROSS-CHECKING
A forward and backward motion with both fists clenched extending from the chest.

(NOTE 2) When a major penalty is assessed for cross-checking, an automatic game misconduct penalty shall be imposed on the offending player.

(b) When a major penalty is imposed under this rule, an automatic fine of one hundred dollars ($100) shall also be imposed.

Rule 49. Deliberate Injury of Opponents

(a) A match penalty shall be imposed on a player who deliberately injures an opponent in any manner.

(NOTE) Any player wearing tape or any other material on his hands (below the wrist) who cuts or injures an opponent during an altercation shall receive a match penalty under this rule.

(b) In addition to the match penalty, the player shall be automatically suspended from further competition until the Commissioner has ruled on the issue.

(c) No substitute shall be permitted to take the place of the penalized player until five minutes of actual playing time have elapsed from the time the penalty was imposed.

(d) A game misconduct penalty shall be imposed on any player who deliberately injures an official, Manager, Coach or Trainer in any manner and the circumstances shall be reported to the Commissioner for further action.

Rule 50. Delaying the Game

(a) A minor penalty shall be imposed on any player or goalkeeper who delays the game by deliberately shooting or batting the puck with his stick outside the playing area.

(NOTE 1) When the goalkeeper shoots the puck directly (non-deflected) out of the playing surface, except where there is no glass, a penalty shall be assessed for delaying the game.

(NOTE 2) This penalty shall also apply when a player or goalkeeper deliberately bats or shoots the puck with his stick outside the playing area after a stoppage of play.

(b) A minor penalty shall be imposed on any player or goalkeeper who throws or deliberately bats the puck with his hand or stick outside the playing area.

(c) A minor penalty shall be imposed on any player (including the goalkeeper) who delays the game by deliberately displacing a goal post from its normal position. The Referee or Linesmen shall stop play immediately when a goal post has been displaced.

If the goal post is deliberately displaced by a goalkeeper or player during the course of a "breakaway", a penalty shot will be awarded to the non-offending team, which shot shall be taken by the player last in possession of the puck.

(NOTE) A player with a "breakaway" is defined as a player in control of the puck with no opposition between him and the opposing goal and with a reasonable scoring opportunity.

In the event that a goalpost is deliberately displaced by a defending player or goalkeeper, prior to the puck crossing the goal line between the normal position of the goalposts, the Referee, at his discretion, may assess a minor penalty under Rule 50(c) (paragraph 1), a penalty shot under Rule 50(d), or award a goal.

(d) If by reason of insufficient time in the regular playing time or by reason of penalties already imposed, the minor penalty assessed to a player for deliberately displacing his own goal post cannot be served in its entirety within the regular playing time of the game or at any time in overtime, a penalty shot shall be awarded against the offending team.

(e) A bench minor penalty shall be imposed upon any team which, after warning by the Referee to its Captain or Alternate Captain to place the correct number of players on the ice and commence play, fails to comply with the Referee's direction and thereby causes any delay by making additional substitutions, by persisting in having its players off-side, or in any other manner.

Rule 51. Elbowing, Kneeing and Head-Butting

ELBOWING
Tapping the elbow of the "whistle hand" with the opposite hand.

KNEEING
Slapping the knee with palm of hand while keeping both skates on the ice.

(a) A minor or major penalty, at the discretion of the Referee, shall be imposed on any player who uses his elbow or knee in such a manner as to in any way foul an opponent.

(b) When a major penalty is imposed under this rule for a foul resulting in an injury to an opponent, an automatic fine of one hundred dollars ($100) shall also be imposed.

(c) A match penalty shall be imposed on any player who deliberately "head-butts" or attempts to "head-butt" or knees an opponent during an altercation and the circumstances shall be reported to the Commissioner for further action. A substitute player is permitted to replace the penalized player after five minutes playing time has elapsed when the penalty is imposed under Rule 44 – Attempt to Injure or Rule 49 – Deliberate Injury of Opponents.

Rule 52. Face-Offs

(a) The puck shall be "faced-off" by the Referee or the Linesman dropping the puck on the ice between the sticks of the players "facing-off". Players facing-off will stand squarely facing their opponent's end of the rink approximately one stick length apart with the blade of their sticks on the ice.

When the face-off takes place in any of the end face-off circles, the players taking part shall take their position so that they will stand squarely facing their opponent's end of the rink. The sticks of both players facing-off shall have the blade on the ice within the designated white area. The visiting player shall place his stick within the designated white area first.

No other player shall be allowed to enter the face-off circle or come within fifteen feet of the players facing-off the puck and must stand on side on all face-offs.

If a violation of this sub-section of this rule occurs, the Referee or Linesman shall re-face the puck.

(b) If after warning by the Referee or Linesman, either of the players fails to take his proper position for the face-off promptly, the official shall be entitled to face-off the puck notwithstanding such default.

(c) In the conduct of any face-off anywhere on the playing surface, no player facing-off shall make any physical contact with his opponent's body by means of his own body or by his stick except in the course of playing the puck after the face-off has been completed.

For violation of this rule, the Referee shall impose a minor penalty or penalties on the player(s) whose action(s) caused the physical contact.

(NOTE) "Conduct of any face-off" commences when the Referee designates the place of the face-off and he (or the Linesman) takes up his position to drop the puck.

(d) If a player facing-off fails to take his proper position immediately when directed by the official, the official may order him replaced for that face-off by any teammate then on the ice.

No substitution of players shall be permitted until the face-off has been completed and play has resumed except when a penalty is imposed which affects the on-ice strength of either team.

(e) A second violation of any of the provisions of sub-section (a) hereof by the same team during the same face-off shall be penalized with a minor penalty to the player who commits the second violation of the rule. The official must drop the puck twice in order to have a second face-off violation.

During end zone face-offs, all other players on the ice must position their bodies and sticks on their own side of the restraining lines marked on the outer edge of the face-off circles.

If a player other than the player taking the face-off moves into the face-off circle prior to the dropping of the puck, then the offending team's player taking the face-off shall be ejected from the face-off circle.

If a violation of this rule occurs, the Referee or Linesman shall order another face-off, unless the non-offending team wins the draw.

(f) When an infringement of a rule has been committed or a stoppage of play has been caused by any player of the attacking side in the attacking zone, the ensuing face-off shall be made in the neutral zone on the nearest face-off spot.

(NOTE) This includes stoppage of play caused by a player of the attacking side shooting the puck on the back of the defending team's net without any intervening action by the defending team.

(g) When an infringement of a rule has been committed by players of both sides in the play resulting in the stoppage, the ensuing face-off will be made at the place of such infringement or at the place where play is stopped.

(h) When stoppage occurs between the end face-off spots and near end of the rink, the puck shall be faced-off at the end face-off spot on the side where the stoppage occurs unless otherwise expressly provided by these rules.

(i) No face-off shall be made within fifteen feet of the goal or sideboards.

(j) When a goal is illegally scored as a result of a puck being deflected directly off an Official anywhere in the defending zone, the resulting face-off shall be made at the end face-off spot in the defending zone.

(k) When the game is stopped for any reason not specifically covered in the official rules, the puck must be faced-off where it was last played.

(l) The whistle will not be blown by the official to start play. Playing time will commence from the instant the puck is faced-off and will stop when the whistle is blown or a goal is scored.

(m) Following a stoppage of play, should one or both defensemen who are the point players or any player coming from the bench of the attacking team, enter into the attacking zone beyond the outer edge of the corner face-off circle, the ensuing face-off shall take place in the neutral zone near the blue line of the defending team.

Rule 53. Falling on Puck

(a) A minor penalty shall be imposed on a player other than the goalkeeper who deliberately falls on or gathers the puck into his body.

(NOTE) Any player who drops to his knees to block a shot should not be

penalized if the puck is shot under him or becomes lodged in his clothing or equipment but any use of the hands to make the puck unplayable should be penalized promptly.

(b) A minor penalty shall be imposed on a goalkeeper who, when he is in his own goal crease, deliberately falls on or gathers the puck into his body or who holds or places the puck against any part of the goal in such a manner as to cause a stoppage of play unless he is actually being checked by an opponent.

(NOTE) Refer to Rule 74(b) – Puck Must Be Kept In Motion for the Rule governing freezing of the puck by a goalkeeper outside of his crease area.

(c) No defending player, except the goalkeeper, will be permitted to fall on the puck, hold the puck or gather the puck into the body or hands when the puck is within the goal crease.

For infringement of this rule, play shall immediately be stopped and a penalty shot shall be ordered against the offending team, but no other penalty shall be given.

(NOTE) The rule shall be interpreted so that a penalty shot will be awarded only when the puck is in the crease at the instant the offense occurs.

However, in cases where the puck is outside the crease, Rule 53(a) may still apply and a minor penalty may be imposed, even though no penalty shot is awarded.

Rule 54. Fisticuffs

(NOTE) An altercation is a situation involving two players, with at least one to be penalized.

(a) A major penalty shall be imposed on any player who engages in fisticuffs. In addition, a minor or a major and/or a game misconduct penalty, at the discretion of the Referee, shall be imposed on any player involved in fisticuffs. A player deemed to be the instigator of fisticuffs shall be assessed a game misconduct. If such player is wearing a face shield, he shall be assessed an additional minor penalty. These penalties are in addition to any other penalty incurred in the same incident.

NEW

A player who deliberately removes his sweater prior to participating in an altercation shall be assessed a minor penalty for instigation and a game misconduct. This is in addition to other penalties to be assessed to the participants of an altercation.

(b) A minor penalty shall be imposed on a player who, having been struck, shall retaliate with a blow or attempted blow. However, at the discretion of the Referee, a major or a double-minor penalty or a game misconduct penalty may be imposed if such player continues the altercation.

(NOTE 1) It is the intent and purpose of this rule that the Referee shall impose the "major and game misconduct" penalty in all cases where the instigator or retaliator of the fight is the aggressor and is plainly doing so for the purpose of intimidation or punishment.

(NOTE 2) The Referee is provided very wide latitude in the penalties which he may impose under this rule. This is done intentionally to enable him to differentiate between the obvious degrees of responsibility of the participants either for starting the fighting or persisting in continuing the fighting. The discretion provided should be exercised realistically.

(NOTE 3) Referees are directed to employ every means provided by these rules to stop "brawling" and should use this rule and Rules 42(e) and (f) – Abuse of Officials and other Misconduct.

(NOTE 4) Any player wearing tape or any other material on his hands (below the wrist) who cuts or injures an opponent during an altercation will receive a match penalty under Rule 49 – Deliberate Injury of Opponents.

(c) A misconduct or game misconduct penalty shall be imposed on any player involved in fisticuffs off the playing surface or with another player who is off the playing surface.

(d) A game misconduct penalty, at the discretion of the Referee, shall be imposed on any player or goalkeeper who is the first to intervene in an altercation then in progress except when a match penalty is being imposed in the original altercation. This penalty is in addition to any other penalty incurred in the same incident.

(e) When a fight occurs, all players not engaged shall go immediately to the area of their players' bench and in the event the altercation takes place at a players' bench, the players on the ice from that team shall go to their defensive zone.

Failure to comply with the Rule shall, in addition to the other penalties that may be assessed, result in a fine to the team of $1,000 and the Coach of said team in the amount of $1,000.

(f) A game misconduct penalty shall be imposed on any player who is assessed a major penalty for fighting after the original altercation.

Notwithstanding this rule, at the discretion of the Referee, the automatic game misconduct penalty may be waived for a player in the altercation if the opposing player was clearly the instigator of the altercation.

(g) Any teams whose players become involved in an altercation, other than during the periods of the game, shall be fined automatically twenty-five thousand dollars ($25,000) in addition to any other appropriate penalties that may be imposed upon the participating players by supplementary discipline or otherwise.

Any player who would be deemed to be an instigator pursuant to Rule 54(a) at a time other than during the periods of the game shall be suspended automatically for ten (10) games. Such determination may be made by the Referee at the time of the incident or subsequently by the Commissioner or his designee based upon such reports and other information as he deems sufficient, including but not limited to television tapes.

(NOTE) In the case of altercations taking place after the period or game the fine under this rule shall be assessed only in the event that an altercation is commenced after the period or game has terminated.

Rule 55. Goals and Assists

(NOTE) It is the responsibility of the Official Scorer to award goals and assists, and his decision in this respect is final notwithstanding the report of the Referee or any other game official. Such awards shall be made or withheld strictly in accordance with the provisions of this rule. Therefore, it is essential that the Official Scorer be thoroughly familiar with every aspect of this rule, be alert to observe all actions which could affect the making of an award and, above all, the awards must be made or withheld with absolute impartiality.

In case of an obvious error in awarding a goal or an assist which has been announced, it should be corrected promptly but changes should not be made in the official scoring summary after the Referee has signed the Game Report.

(a) A goal shall be scored when the puck shall have been put between the goal posts by the stick of a player of the attacking side, from in front and below the cross bar, and entirely across a red line, the width of the diameter of the goal posts drawn on the ice from one goal post to the other with the goal frame in its proper position.

(b) A goal shall be scored if the puck is put into the goal in any way by a player of the defending side. The player of the attacking side who last played the puck shall be credited with the goal but no assist shall be awarded.

(c) A goal cannot be scored by an attacking player who bats or kicks the puck directly into the net. A goal cannot be scored where an attacking player bats or kicks the puck and it is deflected off any player or goalkeeper into the net.

(d) If the puck shall have been deflected into the goal from the shot of an attacking player by striking any part of the person of a player of the same side, a goal shall be allowed. The player who deflected the puck shall be credited with the goal. The goal shall not be allowed if the puck has been kicked, whether intended or not. In addition, the goal shall not be allowed if the puck has been thrown or otherwise deliberately directed into the goal by any means other than a stick.

WASH-OUT
Both arms swung laterally across the body with palms down. When used by the Referee, it means goal disallowed.

(e) If a goal is scored as a result of being deflected directly into the net off an official, the goal shall not be allowed. Refer to Rule 76 – Puck Striking Official.

(f) Should a player legally propel a puck into the goal crease of the opponent club and the puck should become loose and available to another player of the attacking side, a goal scored on the play shall be legal.

(g) Any goal scored, other than as covered by the official rules, shall not be allowed.

(h) A "goal" shall be credited in the scoring records to a player who shall have propelled the puck into the opponent's goal. Each "goal" shall count one point in the player's record.

(i) When a player scores a goal, an "assist" shall be credited to the player or players taking part in the play immediately preceding the goal, but no more than two assists can be given on any goal. Each "assist" shall count one point in the player's record.

(j) Only one point can be credited to any one player on a goal.

Rule 56. Gross Misconduct

Refer to Rule 29 – Misconduct Penalty

Rule 57. Handling Puck with Hands

(a) If a player, except a goalkeeper, closes his hand on the puck, the play shall be stopped and a minor penalty shall be imposed on him. A goalkeeper who holds the puck with his hands for longer than three seconds shall be given a minor penalty unless he is actually being checked by an opponent.

(b) A goalkeeper must not deliberately hold the puck in any manner which, in the opinion of the Referee, causes a stoppage of play, nor throw the puck forward towards the opponent's net, nor deliberately drop the puck into his pads or onto the goal net, nor deliberately pile up snow or obstacles at or near his net, that in the opinion of the Referee, would tend to prevent the scoring of a goal.

(NOTE) The object of this entire rule is to keep the puck in play continuously and any action taken by the goalkeeper which causes an unnecessary stoppage must be penalized without warning.

(c) The penalty for infringement of this rule by the goalkeeper shall be a minor penalty.

(NOTE) In the case of the puck thrown forward by the goalkeeper being taken by an opponent, the Referee shall

allow the resulting play to be completed, and if goal is scored by the non-offending team, it shall be allowed and no penalty given; but if a goal is not scored, play shall be stopped and a minor penalty shall be imposed against the goalkeeper.

(d) A minor penalty shall be imposed on a player,except the goalkeeper, who, while play is in progress, picks up the puck off the ice with his hand.

If a player, except a goalkeeper, while play is in progress, picks up the puck with his hand from the ice in the goal crease area, the play shall be stopped immediately and a penalty shot shall be awarded to the non-offending team.

(e) A player shall be permitted to stop or "bat" a puck in the air with his open hand, or push it along the ice with his hand, and the play shall not be stopped unless, in the opinion of the Referee, he has deliberately directed the puck to a teammate in any zone other than the defensive zone, in which case the play shall be stopped and the puck faced-off at the spot where the offense occurred. Play will not be stopped for any hand pass by players in their own defensive zone.

(NOTE) The object of this rule is to ensure continuous action and the

Referee should NOT stop play unless he is satisfied that the directing of the puck to a teammate was, in fact, DELIBERATE.

A goal cannot be scored by an attacking player who bats the puck with his hand directly into the net. A goal cannot be scored by an attacking player who bats the puck and it is deflected into the net off any player or goalkeeper.

Rule 58. High Sticks

(a) The carrying of sticks above the normal height of the WAIST of the opponent is prohibited and a minor, double-minor or major penalty may be imposed on a player violating this rule, at the discretion of the Referee.

(b) A goal scored by an attacking player who strikes the puck with his stick which is carried above the height of the crossbar of the goal frame shall not be allowed.

A goal scored by a defending player who strikes the puck with his stick which is carried above the height of the crossbar of the goal frame shall be allowed.

(c) When a player carries or holds any part of his stick above the normal height of the WAIST of the opponent so that injury results the Referee shall:

(1) assess a double-minor penalty when it is

HIGH-STICKING
Holding both fists, clenched, one above the other at the side of the head.

deemed to be accidental in nature by the officials;

(2) assess a major and game-misconduct when the high stick is deemed to be careless by the officials. Refer to Rule 29(f) and 28(b).

When a major penalty is imposed under this rule for a foul resulting in injury to an opponent, an automatic fine of one hundred dollars ($100) shall also be imposed. Also, when a major penalty is imposed under this rule, the player, excluding goalkeepers, shall receive automatically a game misconduct penalty.

(d) Batting the puck above the normal height of the shoulders with the stick is prohibited and when it occurs, there shall be a whistle and ensuing face-off at the spot where the offense occurred or at the spot where the puck is touched when a territorial advantage has been gained by the offending team, unless:

(1) the puck has been batted to an opponent in which case the play shall continue;

(2) a player of the defending side shall bat the puck into his own goal in which case the goal shall be allowed.

(NOTE) When a player bats the puck to an opponent under sub-section 1, the Referee shall give the "washout" signal immediately. Otherwise, he will stop the play.

(e) When either team is below the numerical strength of its opponent and a player of the team of greater numerical strength causes a stoppage of play by striking the puck with his stick above the height of his shoulder, the resulting face-off shall be made at one of the end face-off spots adjacent to the goal of the team causing the stoppage.

HOLDING
Clasping the wrist of the "whistle hand" well in front of the chest.

Rule 59. Holding an Opponent

(a) A minor penalty shall be imposed on a player who holds an opponent with hands or stick or in any other way.

(b) A minor penalty shall be assessed to a player who uses his hand to hold an opponent's stick.

Rule 60. Hooking

(a) A minor penalty shall be imposed on a player who impedes or seeks to impede the progress of an opponent by "hooking" with his stick.

HOOKING
A tugging motion with both arms, as if pulling something toward the stomach.

(b) A major penalty shall be be imposed on any player who injures an opponent by "hooking". When a major penalty is imposed under this rule for a foul resulting in injury to the face or head of an opponent, an automatic fine of one hundred dollars ($100) shall also be imposed.

(NOTE) When a player is checking another in such a way that there is only stick-to-stick contact, such action is neither hooking or holding.

Rule 61. Icing the Puck

(a) For the purpose of this rule, the center red line will divide the ice into halves. Should any player of a team, equal or superior in numerical strength to the opposing team, shoot, bat or deflect the puck from his own half of the ice beyond the goal line of the opposing team, play shall be stopped and the puck faced-off at the end face-off spot of the offending team, unless on the play, the puck shall have entered the net of the opposing team, in which case the goal shall be allowed.

For the purpose of this rule, the point of last contact with the puck by the team in possession shall be used to determine whether icing has occurred or not.

(NOTE 1) If during the period of a delayed whistle due to a foul by a player of the side NOT in possession, the side inpossession "ices" the puck, then the face-off following the stoppage of play shall take place in the neutral zone near the defending blue line of the team icing the puck.

ICING
Linesman's arms folded across the upper chest.

(NOTE 2) When a team is "short-handed" as the result of a penalty and the penalty is about to expire, the decision as to whether there has been an "icing" shall be determined at the instant the penalty expires. The action of the penalized player remaining in the penalty box will not alter the ruling.

WASH-OUT
Both arms swung laterally at shoulder level with palms down. When used by the Linesman, it means no icing or no off-side.

(NOTE 3) For the purpose of interpretation of the rule, "icing the puck" is completed the instant the puck is touched first by a defending player (other than the goalkeeper) after it has crossed the goal line and if in the action of so touching the puck, it is knocked or deflected into the net, it is NO goal.

(NOTE 4) When the puck is shot and rebounds from the body or stick of an opponent in his own half of the ice so as to cross the goal line of the player shooting, it shall not be considered as "icing".

(NOTE 5) Notwithstanding the provisions of the section concerning "batting" the puck in respect to the "icing the puck" rule, the provisions of the final paragraph of Rule 57(e) apply and NO goal can be scored by batting the puck with the hand into the opponent's goal whether intended or not.

(NOTE 6) If while the Linesman has signalled a slow whistle for a clean interception under Rule 71(c), the player intercepting shoots or bats the puck beyond the opponent's goal line in such a manner as to constitute "icing the puck", the Linesman "slow whistle" shall be considered exhausted the instant the puck crosses the blue line and "icing" shall be called in the usual manner.

(b) If a player of the side shooting the puck down the ice who is on-side and eligible to play the puck does so before it is touched by an opposing player, the play shall continue and it shall not be considered a violation of this rule.

(c) If the puck was so shot by a player of a

side below the numerical strength of the opposing team, play shall continue and the face-off shall not take place.

(NOTE) If the team returns to full strength following a shot by one of its players, play shall continue and the face-off shall not take place.

(d) If, however, the puck shall go beyond the goal line in the opposite half of the ice directly from either of the players while facing-off, it shall not be considered a violation of this rule.

(e) If, in the opinion of the Linesman, a player of the opposing team except the goalkeeper is able to play the puck before it passes his goal line, but has not done so, the face-off shall not be allowed and play shall continue. If, in the opinion of the Referee, the defending side intentionally abstains from playing the puck promptly when they are in a position to do so, he shall stop the play and order the resulting face-off on the adjacent corner face-off spot nearest the goal of the team at fault.

(NOTE) The purpose of this section is to enforce continuous action and both Referee and Linesmen should interpret and apply the rule to produce this result.

(f) If the puck touches any part of a player of the opposing side, including his skates or his stick, or if it passes through any part of the goal crease before it reaches the opposing team's goal line, or if it touches any part of the opposing team's goalkeeper, including his skates or his stick, at any time before or after crossing the goal line, it shall not be considered.

(NOTE) If a goalkeeper takes any action to dislodge the puck from the back of the net, icing shall be washed out.

(g) If a goalkeeper has been removed from the playing surface for an extra player (teams at equal or superior in numerical strength), the icing rule shall be in effect if the puck passes through or touches any part of the goal crease before it crosses the goal line.

(h) If the Linesman shall have erred in calling an "icing the puck" infraction (regardless of whether either team is short-handed), the puck shall be faced-off on the center ice face-off spot.

Rule 62. Interference

(a) A minor penalty shall be imposed on a player who interferes with or impedes the progress of an opponent who is not in possession of the puck, or who deliberately knocks a stick out of an opponent's hand, or who prevents a player who has dropped his stick or any other piece of equipment from regaining possession of it, or who knocks or shoots any abandoned or broken stick or illegal puck or other debris towards an opposing puck carrier in a manner that could cause him to be distracted. (See also Rule 81(a).)

(NOTE) The last player to touch the puck, other than the goalkeeper, shall be considered the player in possession. In interpreting this rule, the Referee should make sure which of the players is the one creating the interference. Often, it is the action and movement of the attacking player which causes the interference since the defending players are entitled to "stand their ground" or "shadow" the attacking players. Players of the side in possession shall not be allowed to "run" deliberate interference for the puck carrier.

(b) A minor penalty shall be imposed on any player on the players' bench or on the penalty bench who, by means of his stick or his body, interferes with the movements of the puck or of any opponent on the ice during the progress of the play.

INTERFERENCE
Crossed arms stationary in front of the chest with fists closed.

(c) If when the goalkeeper has been removed from the ice,

any member of his team (including the goalkeeper) not legally on the ice, including the Manager, Coach or Trainer, interferes by means of his body, stick or any other object with the movements of the puck or an opposing player, the Referee shall immediately award a goal to the non-offending team.

(d) When a player in control of the puck on his opponent's side of the center red line and having no other opponent to pass than the goalkeeper is interfered with by a stick or any part thereof or any other object thrown or shot by any member of the defending team including the Manager, Coach or Trainer, a penalty shot shall be awarded to the non-offending team.

(NOTE) The attention of Referees is directed particularly to three types of offensive interference which should be penalized:

(1) When the defending team secures possession of the puck in its own end and the other players of that team run interference for the puck carrier by forming a protective screen against forecheckers;

(2) When a player facing-off obstructs his opposing number after the face-off when the opponent is not in possession of the puck;

(3) *When the puck carrier makes a drop pass and follows through so as to make bodily contact with an opposing player.*

Defensive interference consists of bodily contact with an opposing player who is not in possession of the puck.

Rule 63. Interference by/with Spectators

(a) In the event of a player being held or interfered with by a spectator, the Referee or Linesman shall blow the whistle and play shall be stopped unless the team of the player interfered with is in possession of the puck at this time when the play shall be allowed to be completed before blowing the whistle and the puck shall be faced-off at the spot where last played at time of stoppage.

(b) Any player who physically interferes with the spectators shall automatically incur a gross misconduct penalty and the Referee shall report all such infractions to the Commissioner who shall have full power to impose such further penalty as he shall deem appropriate.

(c) In the event that objects are thrown on the ice which interfere with the progress of the game, the Referee shall blow the whistle and stop the play and the puck shall be faced-off at the spot play is stopped.

(NOTE) The Referee shall report to the Commissioner for disciplinary action all cases in which a player becomes involved in an altercation with a spectator.

Rule 64. Kicking a Player

A match penalty shall be imposed on any player who kicks or attempts to kick another player.

Whether or not an injury occurs, the Referee may, at his own discretion, impose a five minute time penalty under this rule. Refer to Rule 44 – Attempt to Injure or Rule 49 – Deliberate Injury of an Opponent.

Rule 65. Kicking the Puck

Kicking the puck shall be permitted in all zones. A goal cannot be scored by an attacking player who kicks the puck directly into the net, whether intended or not. A goal cannot be scored by an attacking player who kicks the puck and it is deflected into the net off any player, goalkeeper or Official.

Rule 66. Leaving Players' or Penalty Bench

(a) No player may leave the players' or penalty bench at any time during an altercation or for the purpose of starting an altercation. Substitutions made prior to the altercation shall be permitted, provided the players so substituting do not enter the altercation.

(b) For violation of this rule, a game misconduct penalty shall be imposed on the player who was the first or second player to leave the players' or penalty bench from either or both teams.

(c) The first player to leave the players' or penalty bench from either or both teams shall be suspended automatically without pay for the next ten (10) regular League and/or playoff games of his team.

(d) The second player to leave the bench from either or both teams shall be suspended automatically without pay for the next five (5) regular League and/or playoff games.

(NOTE) The determination as to the players penalized under (c) and (d) of this rule shall be made by the Referee in consultation with the Linesmen and off-ice officials. In the event that he is unable to identify the offending players, the matter will be

referred to the Commissioner or his designee and such determinations may be made subsequently based on reports and other information including but not limited to television tapes.

(e) Any team that has a player penalized under (a) shall be fined ten thousand dollars ($10,000) for the first instance. This fine shall be increased by five thousand dollars ($5000) for each subsequent occurrence over the next following three-year period.

(f) All players including the first and second players who leave the bench during an altercation shall be subject to an automatic fine in the amount equal to the maximum permitted under the collective bargaining agreement.

(g) Any player who leaves the penalty bench during an altercation and is not the first player, shall be suspended automatically without pay for the next five (5) regular League and/or playoff games.

(h) Except at the end of each period or on expiration of his penalty, no player may, at any time, leave the penalty bench.

(i) A penalized player who leaves the penalty bench before his penalty has expired, whether play is in progress or not, shall incur an additional minor penalty, after serving his unexpired penalty.

(j) Any penalized player leaving the penalty bench during stoppage of play and during an altercation shall incur a minor penalty plus a game misconduct penalty after serving his unexpired time.

(k) If a player leaves the penalty bench before his penalty is fully served, the Penalty Timekeeper shall note the time and signal the Referee who will immediately stop play.

(l) In the case of a player returning to the ice before his time has expired through an error of the Penalty Timekeeper, he is not to serve an additional penalty, but must serve his unexpired time.

(m) If a player of the attacking side in possession of the puck shall be in such a position as to have no opposition between him and the opposing goalkeeper, and while in such position he shall be interfered with by a player of the opposing side who shall have illegally entered the game, the Referee shall impose a penalty shot against the side to which the offending player belongs.

(n) If the opposing goalkeeper has been removed and an attacking player in possession of the puck shall have no player of the defending team to pass and a stick or a part thereof or any other object is thrown or shot by an opposing player, or the player is fouled from behind thereby being prevented from having a clear shot on an open goal, a goal shall be awarded against the offending team.

If when the opposing goalkeeper has been removed from the ice, a player of the side attacking the unattended goal is interfered with by a player who shall have entered the game illegally, the Referee shall immediately award a goal to the non-offending team.

(o) If a Coach or Manager gets on the ice after the start of a period and before that period is ended, the Referee shall impose a bench minor penalty against the team and report the incident to the Commissioner for disciplinary action.

(p) Any club executive or Manager committing the same offense will be automatically fined two hundred dollars ($200).

(q) If a penalized player returns to the ice from the penalty bench before his penalty has expired by his own error or the error of the Penalty Timekeeper, any goal scored by his own team while he is illegally on the ice shall be disallowed but all penalties imposed on either team shall be served as regular penalties.

(r) If a player shall illegally enter the game from his own players' bench or from the penalty bench, any goal scored by his own team while he is illegally on the ice shall be disallowed but all penalties imposed on either team shall be served as regular penalties.

(s) A bench minor penalty shall be imposed on a team whose player(s) leave the players' bench for any purpose other than a change of players and when no altercation is in progress.

(t) Any player who has been ordered to the dressing room by the Referee and returns to his bench or to the ice for any reason before the appropriate time shall be assessed a game misconduct penalty and shall be suspended automatically without pay for the next ten (10) regular League and/or playoff games.

(u) The Coach of the team whose player was the first to leave the players' bench during an altercation shall be suspended automatically for the next five (5) regular League and/or playoff games of his club and shall be fined one thousand dollars ($1,000). The Coach of the team whose players came off the bench subsequently shall be suspended automatically for the next three (3) regular League and/or playoff games of his club and shall be fined one thousand dollars ($1,000). For each subsequent offense of this rule by either or both Coaches over a three-year period, the fines and suspensions shall be doubled.

(v) For all suspensions imposed on players under this rule, the club of the player shall pay to the League a sum equal to the pro-rata of that player's salary covered by the suspension. For purposes of computing amounts due for a player's suspension, the player's fixed salary shall be divided by the number of days in the regular season and then, said result shall be multiplied by the number of games suspended.

In addition, any club that is deemed by the Commissioner to pay or reimburse to the player the amount of the fine or loss of salary assessed under this rule shall be fined automatically one hundred thousand dollars ($100,000).

(NOTE) In the event that suspensions imposed under this rule cannot be completed in regular League and/or playoff games in any one season, the remainder of the suspension shall be served the following season.

Rule 67. Physical Abuse of Officials

(a) Any player who deliberately applies physical force in any manner against an official, in any manner attempts to injure an official, deliberately makes contact with an official, physically demeans an official or deliberately applies physical force to an official solely for the purpose of getting free of such an official during or immediately following an altercation shall receive a game misconduct penalty.

In addition, the following disciplinary penalties shall apply:

CATEGORY I

Any player who deliberately strikes an official and causes injury or who deliberately applies physical force in any manner against an official with intent to injure, or who in any manner attempts to injure an official shall be automatically suspended for not less than 20 games. (For the purpose of the rule, "intent to injure" shall mean any physical force which a player knew or should have known could reasonably be expected to cause injury.)

CATEGORY II

Any player who deliberately applies physical force to an official in any manner (excluding actions as set out in Category One), which physical force is applied without intent to injure, shall be automatically suspended for not less than 10 games.

CATEGORY III

Any player who, by his actions, physically demeans an official or who deliberately applies physical force to an official solely for the purpose of getting free of such an official during or immediately following an altercation shall be suspended for not less than 3 games.

Immediately after the game in which such game misconduct penalty is imposed, the Referee shall, in consultation with the Linesmen, decide the category of the offense. He shall make an oral report to the Commissioner and advise of the category and of the offense. In addition, he shall file a written report to the Commissioner in which he may request a review as to the adequacy of the suspension. The player and club involved shall be notified of the decision of the Referee on the morning following the game and the player may request the Commissioner to review, subject to the provisions of this rule, the penalty imposed by the Referee. Such request must be filed with the Commissioner in writing not later than 72 hours following notification of the penalty. No appeal to the Board of Governors pursuant to By-Law 17 shall be available to the player unless a review has been conducted as provided herein.

If a review of the incident is requested by either the player or by the official, a hearing will be conducted by the Commissioner as soon as practical prior to the fourth game of any suspension. The player's suspension shall continue pending the outcome of the hearing by the Commissioner.

After any review as called for hereby, the Commissioner shall issue an order either:

(1) sustaining the minimum suspension, or . . .

(2) increasing the number of games within the category, or . . .

(3) changing to a lower category, or . . .

(4) changing to a lower category and increasing the number of games within the category.

A player shall have the right of appeal from any such order pursuant to By-Law 17.11. Upon such appeal, the Board of Governors' determination shall be one of the four alternatives listed above.

The penalties imposed under this rule shall not be deemed to limit the right of the Commissioner with respect to any action that he might otherwise take under By-Law 17.

In the event that the player has committed more than one offense under this rule, in addition to the penalties imposed under this offense, his case shall be referred to the Commissioner of the League for consideration of supplementary disciplinary action.

(In all instances where the Commissioner is referred to in this rule, it shall mean the Commissioner or his designee.)

(b) Any club executive, Manager, Coach or Trainer who holds or strikes an official shall be automatically suspended from the game, ordered to the dressing room and a substantial fine shall be imposed by the Commissioner.

Rule 68. Obscene or Profane Language or Gestures

(a) Players shall not use obscene gestures on the ice or anywhere in the rink before, during or after the game. For a violation of the rule, a game misconduct penalty shall be imposed and the Referee shall report the circumstances to the Commissioner of the League for further disciplinary action.

(b) Players shall not use profane language on the ice or anywhere in the rink before, during or after a game. For violation of this rule, a misconduct penalty shall be imposed except when the violation occurs in the vicinity of the players' bench in which case a bench minor penalty shall be imposed.

(NOTE) It is the responsibility of all game officials and all club officials to send a confidential report to the Commissioner setting out the full details concerning the use of obscene gestures or language by any player, Coach or other official. The Commissioner shall take such further disciplinary action as he shall deem appropriate.

(c) Club executives, Managers, Coaches and Trainers shall not use obscene or profane language or gestures anywhere in the rink. For violation of this rule, a bench minor penalty shall be imposed.

Rule 69. Off-Sides

(a) The position of the player's skates and not that of his stick shall be the determining factor in all instances in deciding an "off-side". A player is off-side when both skates are completely over the outer edge of the determining center line or blue line involved in the play.

(NOTE 1) A player is "on-side" when either of his skates are in contact with or on his own side of the line at the instant the puck completely crosses the outer edge of that line regardless of the position of his stick. However, if while an off-side call is delayed, players of the offending team clear the zone, the Linesman shall drop his arm and the play is no longer off-side.

(NOTE 2) It should be noted that while the position of the player's skates is what determines whether a player is "off-side", nevertheless the question of an "off-side" never arises until the puck has completely crossed the outer edge of the line at which time the decision is to be made.

WASH-OUT
Both arms swung laterally at shoulder level with palms down. When used by the Linesman, it means no icing or no off-side.

(b) If in the opinion of the Linesman, an intentional off-side play has been made, the puck shall be faced-off at the end face-off spot in the defending zone of the offending team.

(NOTE 1) An intentional off-side is one which is made for the purpose of securing a stoppage of play regardless of the reason, whether either team is short-handed.

(NOTE 2) If, while an off-side call is delayed, a player of the offending team deliberately touches the puck to create a stoppage of play, the Linesman will signal an intentional off-side.

(c) If a Linesman errs in calling an off-side pass infraction (regardless of whether either team is short-handed), the puck shall be faced-off on the center ice face-off spot.

Rule 70. Passes

(a) The puck may be passed by any player to a player of the same side within any one of the three zones into which the ice is divided, but it may not be passed forward from a player in one zone to a player of the same side in another zone, except by players of the defending team who may make and take forward passes from their own defending zone to the center line without incurring an off-side penalty. This forward pass from the defending zone must be completed by the pass receiver who is preceded by the puck across the center line, otherwise the play shall be stopped and the face-off shall be at the point from which the pass was made.

(NOTE 1) The position of the puck and not that of the player's skates shall be the determining factor in deciding from which zone the pass was made.

(NOTE 2) Passes may be completed legally at the center red line in exactly the same manner as passes at the attacking blue line.

(NOTE 3) In the event the player has preceded the puck at the center line he may become eligible to play the puck if he makes skate contact with the line prior to playing the puck.

(b) Should the puck having been passed, contact any part of the body, stick or skates of a player of the same side who is legally on-side, the pass shall be considered to have been completed.

(c) The player last touched by the puck shall be deemed to be in possession.

Rebounds off goalkeepers' pads or other equipment shall not be considered as a change of possession or completion of the play by the team when applying Rule 34(b) – Calling of Penalties.

(d) If a player in the neutral zone is preceded in the attacking zone by the puck passed from the neutral zone, he shall be eligible to take possession of the puck anywhere in the attacking zone except when the "icing the Puck" rule applies.

(e) If a player in the same zone from which a pass is made is preceded by the puck into succeeding zones, he shall be eligible to take possession of the puck in that zone except where the "icing the Puck" rule applies.

(f) If an attacking player passes the puck backward toward his own goal from the attacking zone, an opponent may play the puck anywhere regardless of whether the opponent was in the same zone at the time the puck was passed. (No "slow whistle".)

Rule 71. Preceding Puck into Attacking Zone

(a) Players of the attacking team must not precede the puck into the attacking zone.

(b) For violation of this rule, the play is

stopped and the puck shall be faced-off in the neutral zone at the face-off spot nearest the attacking zone of the offending team.

(NOTE) A player actually controlling the puck who shall cross the line ahead of the puck shall not be considered "off-side".

(c) If however, notwithstand-ing the fact that a member of the attacking team shall have preceded the puck into the attacking zone, the puck is cleanly intercepted by a member of the defending team at or near the blue line and is carried out or passed by them into the neutral zone, the "off-side" shall be ignored and play permitted to continue. (Officials will carry out this rule by means of the "slow whistle".)

SLOW WHISTLE
Arm in which the whistle is not held extended above head. If play returns to neutral zone without stoppage of play, arm is drawn down the instant the puck crosses the line.

(d) If a player legally carries or passes the puck back into his own defending zone while a player of the opposing team is in such defending zone, the "off-side" shall be ignored and play permitted to continue. (No "slow whistle".)

(NOTE) If a puck clearly deflects off a defending player in the neutral zone, back into the defending zone, all attacking players are eligible to play the puck.

Rule 72. Protection of Goalkeeper

(a) A minor penalty for interference shall be imposed on a player who, by means of his stick or his body, interferes with or impedes the movements of the goalkeeper by actual physical contact.

(NOTE) A goalkeeper is not "fair game" just because he is outside the goal crease area. A penalty for interference or charging (minor or major) should be called in every case where an opposing player makes unnecessary contact with the goalkeeper.

Likewise, referees should be alert to penalize goalkeepers for tripping, slashing, or spearing in the vicinity of the goal.

(b) Unless the puck is in the goal crease area, a player of the attacking side may not stand in the goal crease. If the puck should enter the net while such conditions prevail the goal shall not be allowed. If an attacking player has physically interfered with the goalkeeper, prior to or during the scoring of the goal, the goal will be disallowed and a penalty for goaltender interference will be assessed. The ensuing face-off shall be taken in the neutral zone at the face-off spot nearest the attacking zone of the offending team.

(c) If a player of the attacking side has been physically interfered with by the action of any defending player so as to cause him to be in the goal crease and the puck should enter the net while the player so interfered with is still in the goal crease, the goal shall be allowed.

(d) A minor penalty shall be assessed to a player of the attacking side who having been interfered with fails to avoid making contact with the goalkeeper. In addition, if a goal is scored it shall be disallowed.

(e) A minor penalty for interference shall be imposed on any attacking player, who makes deliberate contact with a goalkeeper whether in or out of the crease. At the discretion of the Referee a major penalty may be imposed under Rule 47(c) – Charging.

(f) A minor and misconduct penalty shall be imposed on an attacking player, not in possession of the puck, who is tripped or caused to fall and fails to attempt to avoid contact with the goalkeeper whether he is in or out of his crease.

(g) In the event that a goalkeeper has been pushed into the net together with the puck after making the stop, the goal will be disallowed. If applicable, the appropriate penalties will be assessed.

Rule 73. Puck Out of Bounds or Unplayable

(a) When the puck goes outside the playing area at either end or either side of the rink, or strikes any obstacles above the playing surface other than the boards or glass, it shall be faced-off from where it was shot or deflected unless otherwise expressly provided in these rules.

(b) When the puck becomes lodged in the netting on the outside of either goal so as to make it unplayable, or if it is frozen between opposing players intentionally or otherwise, the Referee shall stop the play and face-off the puck at either of the adjacent face-off spots unless in the opinion of the Referee, the stoppage was caused by a player of the attacking team, in which case the resulting face-off shall be conducted in the neutral zone.

(NOTE) This includes a stoppage of play caused by a player of the attacking side shooting the puck onto

the back of the defending team's net without any intervening action by the defending team.

The defending team and/or the attacking team may play the puck off the net at any time. However, should the puck remain on the net for more than three seconds, play shall be stopped and the face-off shall take place in the end face-off zone except when the stoppage is caused by the attacking team, then the face-off shall take place on a face-off spot in the neutral zone.

(c) A minor penalty shall be imposed on a goalkeeper who deliberately drops the puck on the goal netting to cause a stoppage of play.

(d) If the puck comes to rest on top of the boards surrounding the playing area, it shall be considered to be in play and may be played legally by hand or stick.

Rule 74. Puck Must Be Kept in Motion

(a) The puck must at all times be kept in motion.

(b) A minor penalty shall be imposed on any player, including the goalkeeper, who holds, freezes or plays the puck with his stick, skates or body in such a manner as to deliberately cause a stoppage of play.

(NOTE) With regard to a goalkeeper, this rule applies outside of his goal crease area.

Rule 75. Puck Out of Sight and Illegal Puck

(a) Should a scramble take place or a player accidentally fall on the puck and the puck be out of sight of the Referee, he shall immediately blow his whistle and stop the play. The puck shall then be faced-off at the point where the play was stopped unless otherwise provided for in the rules.

(b) If at any time while play is in progress, a puck other than the one legally in play shall appear on the playing surface, the play shall not be stopped but shall continue with the legal puck until the play then in progress is completed by change of possession.

Rule 76. Puck Striking Official

Play shall not be stopped if the puck touches an official anywhere on the rink, regardless of whether a team is shorthanded or not. A puck that deflects back into the defensive zone, off an official who is in the neutral zone, may be deemed to be off-side as per Rule 69

(Note 1) Off-Sides. If a goal is scored as a result of being deflected directly into the net off an official the goal shall not be allowed.

Rule 77. Refusing to Start Play

(a) If when both teams are on the ice, one team for any reason shall refuse to play when ordered to do so by the Referee, he shall warn the Captain and allow the team so refusing fifteen seconds within which to begin the play or resume play. If at the end of that time, the team shall still refuse to play, the Referee shall impose a two-minute penalty on a player of the offending team to be designated by the Manager or Coach of that team through the playing Captain. Should there be a repetition of the same incident, the Referee shall notify the Manager or Coach that he has been fined the sum of two hundred dollars ($200). Should the offending team still refuse to play, the Referee shall have no alternative but to declare that the game be forfeited to the non-offending club and the case shall be reported to the Commissioner for further action.

(b) If a team, when ordered to do so by the Referee through its club executive, Manager or Coach, fails to go on the ice and start play within five minutes, the club executive, Manager or Coach shall be fined five hundred dollars ($500), the game shall be forfeited and the case shall be reported to the Commissioner for further action.

(NOTE) The Commissioner of the League shall issue instructions pertaining to records, etc., of a forfeited game.

Rule 78. Slashing

(a) A minor or major penalty, at the discretion of the Referee, shall be imposed on any player who impedes or seeks to impede the progress of an opponent by "slashing" with his stick.

(b) A major and a game misconduct penalty shall be imposed on any player who injures an opponent by slashing. In addition, a fine of one hundred dollars ($100) shall be imposed for each major penalty assessed under this rule.

(NOTE) Referees should penalize as "slashing" any player who swings his stick at any opposing

SLASHING
A chopping motion with the edge of one hand across the opposite forearm.

player (whether in or out of range) without actually striking him or where a player, on the pretext of playing the puck, makes a wild swing at the puck with the object of intimidating an opponent.

(c) Any player who swings his stick at another player in the course of an altercation shall be subject to a fine of not less than two hundred dollars ($200), with or without suspension, to be imposed by the Commissioner.

(NOTE) The Referee shall impose the normal appropriate penalty provided in the other sections of this rule and shall, in addition, report promptly to the Commissioner all infractions under this section.

Rule 79. Spearing and Butt-Ending

(a) A major penalty and a game misconduct penalty shall be imposed on a player who spears or butt-ends an opponent.

(b) In addition to the major penalty imposed under this rule, an automatic fine of one hundred dollars ($100) will also be imposed.

SPEARING
A jabbing motion with both hands thrust out in front of the body.

(NOTE 1) "Spearing" shall mean stabbing an opponent with the point of the stick blade while the stick is being carried with one or both hands.

(NOTE 2) "Butt-ending" shall mean using the end of the shaft of the stick in a jabbing motion.

(NOTE 3) "Spearing" and "Butt-ending" may also be treated as a deliberate attempt to injure under Rule 44.

(c) A double-minor penalty will be imposed by the officials on a player who attempts to spear, poke, jab or butt-end an opponent.

(NOTE) Attempts to spear or butt-end will include all cases where a gesture is made without contact.

Rule 80. Start of Game and Periods

(a) The game shall be commenced at the time scheduled by a "face-off" in the center of the rink and shall be renewed promptly at the conclusion of each intermission in the same manner.

No delay shall be permitted by reason of any ceremony, exhibition, demonstration or presentation unless consented to reasonably in advance by the visiting team.

(b) Home clubs shall have the choice of goals to defend at the start of the game except where both players' benches are on the same side of the rink, in which case the home club shall start the game defending the goal nearest to its own bench. The teams shall change ends for each period of regulation time and, in the playoffs, for each period of overtime. (See Rule 83(a) – NOTE – Tied Games)

(c) During the pre-game warm-up (which shall not exceed twenty minutes in duration) and before the commencement of play in any period, each team shall confine its activity to its own end of the rink. Refer to Rule 54(g) – Fisticuffs.

(NOTE 1) The Game Timekeeper shall be responsible for signalling the commencement and termination of the pre-game warm-up and any violation of this rule by the players shall be reported to the Commissioner by the supervisor when in attendance at the game.

(NOTE 2) Players shall not be permitted to come on the ice during a stoppage of play or at the end of the first and second periods for the purpose of warming-up. The Referee will report any violation of this rule to the Commissioner for disciplinary action.

(d) Twenty minutes before the time scheduled for the start of the game, both teams shall vacate the ice and proceed to their dressing rooms while the ice is being flooded. Both teams shall be signalled by the Game Timekeeper to return to the ice together in time for the scheduled start of the game.

(e) At the beginning of the game, if a team fails to appear on the ice promptly without proper justification, a fine shall be assessed against the offending team, the amount of the fine to be decided by the Commissioner.

At the beginning of the second and third periods, and overtime periods in playoffs (0:00 on the clock), clubs must be on the ice or be observed to be proceeding to the ice. For failure to comply, a bench minor penalty for delay of game shall be imposed.

(f) At the end of each period, the home team players must proceed directly to their dressing room while the visiting team players must wait for a signal from the Referee to proceed only if they have to go on the ice to reach their dressing room. Failure to comply with this regulation will result in a two-minute bench minor for delay of game.

Rule 81. Throwing Stick

(a) When any player of the defending side or Manager, Coach or Trainer, deliberately throws or shoots a stick or any part thereof or any other object at the puck in his defending zone, the Referee shall allow the play to be completed and if a goal is not scored, a penalty shot shall be awarded to the non-offending side, which shot shall be taken by the player designated by the Referee as the player fouled.

If however, the goal being unattended and the attacking player having no defending player to pass and having a chance to score on an "open net", a stick or any part thereof or any other object be thrown or shot by a member of the defending team, including the Manager, Coach or Trainer, thereby preventing a shot on the "open net", a goal shall be awarded to the attacking side.

(NOTE 1) If the officials are unable to determine the person against whom the offense was made, the offended team, through the Captain, shall designate a player on the ice at the time the offense was committed to take the shot.

(NOTE 2) For the purpose of this rule, an open net is defined as one from

which a goalkeeper has been removed for an additional attacking player.

(b) A major penalty shall be imposed on any player on the ice who throws his stick or any part thereof or any other object in the direction of the puck in any zone, except when such act has been penalized by the assessment of a penalty shot or the award of a goal.

(NOTE) When the player discards the broken portion of a stick by tossing it to the side of the ice (and not over the boards) in such a way as will not interfere with play or opposing player, no penalty will be imposed for so doing.

(c) A misconduct or game misconduct penalty, at the discretion of the Referee, shall be imposed on a player who throws his stick or any part thereof outside the playing area. If the offense is committed in protest of an official's decision, a minor penalty for unsportsmanlike conduct plus a game misconduct penalty shall be assessed to the offending player.

Rule 82. Time of Match

(a) The time allowed for a game shall be three twenty-minute periods of actual play with a rest intermission between periods.

Play shall be resumed promptly following each intermission upon the expiry of fifteen minutes from the completion of play in the preceding period. A preliminary warning shall be given by the Game Timekeeper to the officials and to both teams five minutes prior to the resumption of play in each period and the final warning shall be given two minutes prior to resumption of play to enable the teams to start play promptly.

(NOTE) For the purpose of keeping the spectators informed as to the time remaining during intermissions, the Game Timekeeper will use the electric clock to record length of intermissions.

(b) The team scoring the greatest number of goals during the three twenty-minute periods shall be the winner and shall be credited with two points in the League standing.

(c) In the interval between periods, the ice surface shall be flooded unless mutually agreed to the contrary.

(d) If any unusual delay occurs within five minutes of the end of the first or second periods, the Referee may order the next regular intermission to be taken immediately and the balance of the period will be completed on the resumption of play with the teams defending the same goals after which, the teams will change ends and resume play of the ensuing period without delay.

(NOTE) If a delay takes place with more than five minutes remaining in the first or second period, the Referee will order the next regular intermission to be taken immediately only when requested to do so by the home club.

Rule 83. Tied Games

156(a)If at the end of the three regular twenty-minute periods the score shall be tied, the teams will play an additional period of not more than five (5) minutes with the team scoring first being declared the winner. If at the end of the overtime period, the score remains tied, each team shall be credited with one point in the League standing.

(NOTE) The overtime period will be commenced immediately following a two-minute rest period during which the players will remain on the ice. The teams will not change ends for the overtime period.

(b) Special conditions for the duration and number of periods of Playoff games shall be arranged by the Board of Governors.

Rule 84. Tripping

(a) A minor penalty shall be imposed on any player who shall place his stick, knee, foot, arm, hand or elbow in such a manner that it shall cause his opponent to trip or fall.

(NOTE 1) If in the opinion of the Referee, a player is unquestionably hook-checking the puck and obtains possession of it thereby tripping the puck carrier, no penalty shall be imposed.

(NOTE 2) Accidental trips occurring simultaneously with or after a stoppage of play will not be penalized.

(b) When a player, in control of the puck on the opponent's side of the center red line and having no other opponent to pass than the goalkeeper, is tripped or otherwise fouled from behind thus preventing a reasonable scoring opportunity, a penalty shot shall be awarded to the non-offending side. Nevertheless, the Referee shall not stop play until the attacking side has lost possession of the puck to the defending side.

TRIPPING
Strike the right leg with the right hand below the knee keeping both skates on the ice.

(NOTE) The intention of this rule is to restore a reasonable scoring opportunity which has been lost by reason of a foul from behind when the foul is committed on the opponent's side of the center red line.

"Control of the puck" means the act of propelling the puck with the stick. If while it is being propelled, the puck is touched by another player or his equipment, hits the goal or goes free, the player shall no longer be considered to be "in control of the puck".

(c) If, when the opposing goalkeeper has been removed from the ice, a player in control of the puck is tripped or otherwise fouled with no opposition between him and the opposing goal thus preventing a reasonable scoring opportunity, the Referee shall immediately stop the play and award a goal to the attacking team.

ROUGHING
A thrusting motion with the arm extending from the side.

Rule 85. Unnecessary Roughness

At the discretion of the Referee, a minor penalty or a double-minor penalty may be imposed on any player deemed guilty of unnecessary roughness.

Rule 86. Time-Outs

Each team shall be permitted to take one thirty-second time-out during the course of any game, regular-season or playoffs. This time-out must be taken during a normal stoppage of play. Any player designated by the Coach will indicate to the Referee that his team is exercising its option and the Referee will report the time-out to the Game Timekeeper who shall be responsible for signalling the termination of the time-out.

(NOTE 1) All players including goalkeepers on the ice at the time of the time-out will be allowed to go to their respective benches. Only one team is allowed a time-out per stoppage and no time-out will be allowed after a reasonable amount of time has elapsed during a normal stoppage of play.

(NOTE 2) For the purposes of this rule, a commercial stoppage in play is deemed to be an "official time-out" and not charged to either team.

Rule 87. Video Goal Judge

The following situations are subject to review by the Video Goal Judge:

(a) Puck crossing the goal line.

(b) Puck in the net prior to the goal frame being dislodged.

(c) Puck in the net prior to, or after expiration of time at the end of the period.

(d) Puck directed into the net by a hand or foot.

(e) Puck deflected into the net off an official.

(f) Puck struck with a high-stick, above the height of the crossbar, by an attacking player prior to entering the goal.

NEW

(g) To establish the correct time on the official game clock, provided the game time is visible on the Video Goal Judge's monitors.

NHL Schedule, 1994-95

GAME #	VISITOR	HOME
Sat. Oct. 1		
1	CHI	PIT
2	WPG	OTT
3	BOS	MTL
4	BUF	QUE
5	T.B.	NYI
6	NYR	N.J.
7	HFD	PHI
8	WSH	TOR
9	ST.L.	DET
10	ANA	DAL
11	VAN	CGY
12	L.A.	S.J.
Sun. Oct. 2		
13	ST.L.	CHI
14	VAN	EDM
Mon. Oct. 3		
15	BOS	OTT
16	PIT	NYR
Tue. Oct. 4		
17	QUE	T.B.
18	PHI	FLA
19	HFD	TOR
20	CGY	DAL
Wed. Oct. 5		
21	BUF	PIT
22	WSH	OTT
23	MTL	WPG
24	ANA	EDM
25	S.J.	VAN
26	DET	L.A.
Thur. Oct. 6		
27	QUE	BOS
28	PHI	NYR
29	N.J.	CHI
30	ST.L.	FLA
Fri. Oct. 7		
31	MTL	BUF
32	OTT	NYI
33	PIT	WSH
34	ST.L.	T.B.
35	EDM	WPG
36	ANA	VAN
37	DET	S.J.
Sat. Oct. 8		
38	TOR	BOS
39	QUE	HFD
40	BUF	MTL
41	OTT	N.J.
42	T.B.	PHI
43	NYI	WSH
44	* NYR	FLA
45	CHI	DAL
46	CGY	L.A.
Sun. Oct. 9		
47	EDM	CHI
48	* VAN	S.J.
49	CGY	ANA
Mon. Oct. 10		
50	* FLA	BOS
51	TOR	BUF
Tue. Oct. 11		
52	PIT	QUE
53	T.B.	NYR
54	OTT	TOR
55	CHI	ST.L.
56	WPG	DAL
57	S.J.	L.A.
Wed. Oct. 12		
58	FLA	HFD
59	WSH	PIT
60	NYI	MTL
61	PHI	N.J.
62	BUF	DET
63	CGY	EDM
64	BOS	S.J.
65	VAN	ANA
Thur. Oct. 13		
66	QUE	TOR
67	WPG	CHI
68	NYR	ST.L.
69	VAN	L.A.
Fri. Oct. 14		
70	HFD	BUF
71	MTL	WSH
72	FLA	DET
73	PHI	WPG
74	S.J.	CGY
75	BOS	ANA
Sat. Oct. 15		
76	NYR	HFD
77	MTL	PIT
78	CHI	QUE
79	DET	NYI
80	BUF	WSH
81	N.J.	T.B.
82	ST.L.	TOR
83	OTT	DAL
84	EDM	VAN
85	BOS	L.A.
Sun. Oct. 16		
86	N.J.	FLA
87	T.B.	ST.L.
88	S.J.	WPG
89	PHI	CGY

OCTOBER 17 – NOVEMBER 1, 1994

GAME #	VISITOR	HOME
Mon. Oct. 17		
90	CHI	MTL
91	DAL	DET
92	PHI	VAN
93	EDM	ANA
Tue. Oct. 18		
94	NYR	QUE
95	L.A.	NYI
96	PIT	T.B.
97	S.J.	ST.L.
98	WPG	CGY
Wed. Oct. 19		
99	OTT	HFD
100	WSH	N.J.
101	TOR	FLA
102	MTL	DET
103	DAL	WPG
104	ANA	EDM
105	BOS	VAN
Thur. Oct. 20		
106	L.A.	NYR
107	QUE	PHI
108	TOR	T.B.
109	S.J.	CHI
110	ANA	CGY
Fri. Oct. 21		
111	FLA	BUF
112	HFD	WSH
113	PIT	DET
114	VAN	DAL
115	BOS	EDM
Sat. Oct. 22		
116	WSH	HFD
117	L.A.	PIT
118	NYR	MTL
119	DET	QUE
120	FLA	NYI
121	*S.J.	N.J.
122	*OTT	PHI
123	TOR	ST.L.
124	CHI	WPG
125	BOS	CGY
Sun. Oct. 23		
126	QUE	BUF
127	*T.B.	OTT
128	S.J.	NYR
129	L.A.	CHI
130	VAN	ST.L.
131	*EDM	DAL
132	ANA	WPG
Mon. Oct. 24		
133	N.J.	MTL
134	CGY	TOR
Tue. Oct. 25		
135	DAL	PIT
136	EDM	QUE
137	VAN	NYI
138	L.A.	FLA
139	ANA	DET
140	WSH	ST.L.
Wed. Oct. 26		
141	PIT	OTT
142	EDM	MTL
143	DAL	NYR
144	CGY	N.J.
145	L.A.	T.B.
Thur. Oct. 27		
146	MTL	BOS
147	QUE	HFD
148	VAN	PHI
149	BUF	FLA
150	ANA	CHI
151	WSH	WPG
Fri. Oct. 28		
152	CGY	NYR
153	EDM	TOR
154	L.A.	DET
Sat. Oct. 29		
155	BUF	BOS
156	WPG	HFD
157	DET	OTT
158	PIT	MTL
159	DAL	QUE
160	CGY	NYI
161	VAN	N.J.
162	TOR	PHI
163	ST.L.	S.J.
Sun. Oct. 30		
164	VAN	NYR
165	WPG	N.J.
166	T.B.	CHI
167	WSH	EDM
168	ST.L.	ANA
Tue. Nov. 1		
169	OTT	PIT
170	T.B.	QUE
171	HFD	DET
172	NYI	DAL
173	WSH	CGY
174	N.J.	S.J.
175	NYR	L.A.

* – afternoon game

NOVEMBER 2 – 18, 1994

GAME #	VISITOR	HOME
Wed. Nov. 2		
176	CHI	BUF
177	PHI	OTT
178	T.B.	MTL
179	NYI	ST.L.
180	TOR	WPG
181	FLA	EDM
182	WSH	VAN
183	NYR	ANA
Thur. Nov. 3		
184	PIT	BOS
Fri. Nov. 4		
185	PHI	BUF
186	TOR	DET
187	WPG	DAL
188	EDM	CGY
189	L.A.	VAN
190	N.J.	ANA
Sat. Nov. 5		
191	CHI	BOS
192	HFD	PIT
193	MTL	OTT
194	BUF	PHI
195	QUE	WSH
196	NYI	T.B.
197	DET	TOR
198	WPG	ST.L.
199	FLA	VAN
200	NYR	S.J.
Sun. Nov. 6		
201	DAL	CHI
202	FLA	CGY
203	N.J.	L.A.
Mon. Nov. 7		
204	BOS	OTT
205	DAL	NYI
206	S.J.	VAN

GAME #	VISITOR	HOME
Tue. Nov. 8		
207	MTL	HFD
208	N.J.	PIT
209	T.B.	BUF
210	PHI	QUE
211	EDM	WSH
212	WPG	DET
213	ST.L.	CGY
214	VAN	S.J.
215	ANA	L.A.
Wed. Nov. 9		
216	HFD	NYR
217	NYI	FLA
218	T.B.	TOR
Thur. Nov. 10		
219	QUE	BOS
220	OTT	BUF
221	MTL	N.J.
222	WSH	PHI
223	TOR	CHI
224	PIT	DAL
225	ST.L.	WPG
226	ANA	S.J.
227	CGY	L.A.
Fri Nov. 11		
228	NYI	NYR
229	EDM	FLA
230	VAN	ANA
Sat. Nov. 12		
231	* OTT	QUE
232	HFD	NYI
233	* BOS	N.J.
234	PHI	WSH
235	EDM	T.B.
236	MTL	TOR
237	PIT	ST.L.
238	DET	DAL
239	CHI	WPG
240	BUF	S.J.
241	VAN	L.A.

GAME #	VISITOR	HOME
Sun. Nov. 13		
242	HFD	OTT
243	* N.J.	QUE
244	WSH	NYR
245	DAL	PHI
246	BOS	FLA
247	ST.L.	CHI
248	CGY	ANA
Mon. Nov. 14		
249	EDM	WPG
Tue. Nov. 15		
250	DAL	WSH
251	CGY	S.J.
252	CHI	L.A.
253	BUF	ANA
Wed. Nov. 16		
254	ST.L.	HFD
255	PIT	OTT
256	NYI	MTL
257	DAL	N.J.
258	DET	T.B.
259	WPG	TOR
260	VAN	EDM
Thur. Nov. 17		
261	ST.L.	BOS
262	OTT	PIT
263	MTL	QUE
264	NYR	PHI
265	DET	FLA
266	ANA	VAN
267	BUF	L.A.
Fri. Nov. 18		
268	NYI	N.J.
269	TOR	WSH
270	WPG	T.B.
271	S.J.	DAL
272	CGY	EDM

NOVEMBER 19 – DECEMBER 4, 1994

GAME #	VISITOR	HOME
Sat. Nov. 19		
273	WSH	BOS
274	NYI	HFD
275	NYR	OTT
276	QUE	MTL
277	PIT	PHI
278	N.J.	T.B.
279	WPG	FLA
280	ST.L.	TOR
281	CGY	VAN
Sun. Nov. 20		
282	DET	PHI
283	S.J.	EDM
284	CHI	ANA
Mon. Nov. 21		
285	PIT	BOS
286	HFD	MTL
287	FLA	QUE
288	VAN	TOR
289	BUF	DAL
Tue. Nov. 22		
290	L.A.	CGY
291	CHI	S.J.
Wed. Nov. 23		
292	PHI	HFD
293	NYR	PIT
294	BOS	BUF
295	N.J.	OTT
296	FLA	MTL
297	T.B.	NYI
298	VAN	WSH
299	ST.L.	DET
300	QUE	DAL
301	TOR	WPG
302	L.A.	EDM
303	S.J.	ANA
Thur. Nov. 24		
304	QUE	ST.L.
305	CHI	CGY

GAME #	VISITOR	HOME
Fri. Nov. 25		
306	* ANA	BOS
307	VAN	BUF
308	* N.J.	PHI
309	PIT	WSH
310	NYR	WPG
311	CHI	EDM
Sat. Nov. 26		
312	* ANA	HFD
313	S.J.	PIT
314	FLA	OTT
315	L.A.	MTL
316	WSH	QUE
317	TOR	NYI
318	* T.B.	PHI
319	* N.J.	DET
320	ST.L.	DAL
321	CGY	EDM
Sun. Nov. 27		
322	* VAN	BOS
323	T.B.	HFD
324	NYI	BUF
325	FLA	NYR
Mon. Nov. 28		
326	L.A.	OTT
327	WSH	MTL
328	S.J.	DET
329	WPG	ST.L.
330	TOR	DAL
Tue. Nov. 29		
331	NYR	HFD
332	ANA	PIT
333	L.A.	QUE
334	BOS	NYI

GAME #	VISITOR	HOME
Wed. Nov. 30		
335	WSH	OTT
336	BUF	NYR
337	FLA	T.B.
338	ANA	TOR
339	PHI	DET
340	MTL	ST.L.
341	WPG	EDM
Thur. Dec. 1		
342	HFD	BOS
343	WSH	PIT
344	QUE	N.J.
345	NYI	PHI
346	S.J.	FLA
347	MTL	CHI
Fri. Dec. 2		
348	L.A.	BUF
349	ANA	NYR
350	S.J.	T.B.
351	CGY	DET
352	DAL	VAN
Sat. Dec. 3		
353	BOS	PIT
354	PHI	OTT
355	DET	MTL
356	HFD	QUE
357	BUF	NYI
358	* EDM	N.J.
359	T.B.	WSH
360	CHI	FLA
361	L.A.	TOR
362	WPG	VAN
Sun. Dec. 4		
363	BOS	HFD
364	CGY	OTT
365	EDM	NYR
366	ANA	CHI
367	N.J.	ST.L.

* – afternoon game

DECEMBER 5 – 19, 1994

GAME #	VISITOR	HOME
Mon. Dec. 5		
368	T.B.	FLA
369	S.J.	DAL
Tue. Dec. 6		
370	NYR	PIT
371	CGY	QUE
372	EDM	NYI
373	BOS	DET
374	TOR	VAN
Wed. Dec. 7		
375	DET	HFD
376	PIT	BUF
377	CGY	MTL
378	OTT	T.B.
379	ST.L.	DAL
380	N.J.	WPG
381	TOR	S.J.
382	WSH	ANA
Thur. Dec. 8		
383	EDM	BOS
384	NYI	NYR
385	MTL	PHI
386	OTT	FLA
387	VAN	CHI
388	WSH	L.A.
Fri. Dec. 9		
389	HFD	BUF
390	DET	N.J.
391	QUE	T.B.
392	CHI	DAL
393	ANA	S.J.
Sat. Dec. 10		
394	CGY	BOS
395	EDM	HFD
396	BUF	PIT
397	PHI	MTL
398	OTT	NYI
399	QUE	FLA
400	DAL	ST.L.
401	VAN	WPG
402	WSH	S.J.
403	TOR	L.A.
Sun. Dec. 11		
404	N.J.	PHI
405	FLA	CHI
406	DET	ST.L.
407	TOR	ANA
Mon. Dec. 12		
408	CGY	HFD
409	L.A.	VAN
Tue. Dec. 13		
410	N.J.	OTT
411	FLA	QUE
412	NYR	NYI
	at Portland	
413	WPG	WSH
414	DAL	DET
415	TOR	EDM
416	PIT	ANA
Wed. Dec. 14		
417	OTT	HFD
418	BOS	MTL
419	BUF	T.B.
420	NYR	VAN
421	DAL	CHI
422	NYI	S.J.
Thur. Dec. 15		
423	FLA	N.J.
424	WPG	PHI
425	QUE	DET
426	TOR	CGY
427	PIT	L.A.
Fri. Dec. 16		
428	MTL	BUF
429	BOS	WSH
430	CHI	T.B.
431	ST.L.	VAN
432	S.J.	ANA
Sat. Dec. 17		
433	BUF	BOS
434	WSH	HFD
435	OTT	MTL
436	* PHI	QUE
437	FLA	TOR
438	* WPG	DET
439	N.J.	DAL
440	NYR	EDM
441	PIT	S.J.
442	NYI	L.A.
Sun. Dec. 18		
443	* T.B.	QUE
444	DET	WPG
445	NYR	CGY
446	PHI	CHI
447	ST.L.	EDM
448	NYI	ANA
Mon. Dec. 19		
449	BUF	OTT
450	T.B.	MTL
451	DAL	TOR

DECEMBER 20, 1994 – JANURAY 6, 1995

GAME #	VISITOR	HOME
Tue. Dec. 20		
452	DET	PIT
453	HFD	N.J.
454	WSH	FLA
455	NYI	CHI
456	ST.L.	CGY
457	EDM	S.J.
Wed. Dec. 21		
458	DAL	HFD
459	T.B.	OTT
460	QUE	PHI
461	BUF	MTL
462	BOS	NYR
463	CHI	TOR
464	ANA	WPG
465	VAN	S.J.
	at Portland	
Thur. Dec. 22		
466	DAL	BOS
467	PIT	FLA
468	ANA	CGY
469	EDM	L.A.
Fri. Dec. 23		
470	HFD	BUF
471	QUE	NYI
472	MTL	NYR
473	OTT	N.J.
474	PHI	WSH
475	PIT	T.B.
476	CHI	DET
477	VAN	ST.L.
Mon. Dec. 26		
478	HFD	BOS
479	WSH	NYI
480	OTT	NYR
481	BUF	N.J.
482	PHI	T.B.
483	DET	CHI
484	ST.L.	DAL
485	L.A.	ANA

GAME #	VISITOR	HOME
Tue. Dec. 27		
486	N.J.	BUF
487	TOR	QUE
488	NYR	WSH
489	PHI	FLA
490	CHI	ST.L.
491	CGY	WPG
492	S.J.	EDM
493	MTL	VAN
Wed. Dec. 28		
494	PIT	HFD
495	NYI	OTT
496	DAL	DET
497	ANA	L.A.
Thur. Dec. 29		
498	BUF	PIT
499	HFD	QUE
500	FLA	WSH
501	DAL	TOR
502	S.J.	ST.L.
503	BOS	WPG
504	CGY	VAN
Fri. Dec. 30		
505	PHI	NYI
506	FLA	N.J.
507	NYR	T.B.
508	MTL	EDM
509	CHI	ANA
Sat. Dec. 31		
510	NYI	PIT
511	PHI	BUF
512	HFD	OTT
513	BOS	TOR
514	S.J.	DET
515	DAL	ST.L.
516	* L.A.	WPG
517	MTL	CGY
518	N.J.	WSH
519	QUE	VAN

GAME #	VISITOR	HOME
Sun. Jan. 1		
520	* NYR	FLA
521	S.J.	CHI
Mon. Jan. 2		
522	* T.B.	BOS
523	OTT	TOR
	at Hamilton	
524	L.A.	DAL
525	* ST.L.	WSH
526	EDM	WPG
	at Saskatoon	
527	* MTL	ANA
Tue. Jan. 3		
528	CHI	NYI
529	ST.L.	NYR
530	VAN	FLA
531	CGY	DET
Wed. Jan. 4		
532	L.A.	HFD
533	PIT	N.J.
534	VAN	T.B.
535	MTL	S.J.
Thur. Jan. 5		
536	PHI	BOS
537	FLA	PIT
538	MTL	QUE
	at Phoenix	
539	NYR	NYI
540	CGY	CHI
541	OTT	WPG
Fri. Jan. 6		
542	VAN	HFD
543	ANA	BUF
544	L.A.	WSH
545	DAL	T.B.
546	CHI	DET

* – afternoon game

JANUARY 7 – 24, 1995

GAME #	VISITOR	HOME
Sat. Jan. 7		
547	DET	BOS
548	BUF	HFD
549	PHI	PIT
	at San Antonio	
550	TOR	OTT
551	WSH	NYI
552	ANA	N.J.
553	NYR	T.B.
554	FLA	ST.L.
555	WPG	DAL
556	QUE	EDM
557	* CGY	S.J.
Sun. Jan. 8		
558	L.A.	CHI
559	WPG	ST.L.
560	QUE	CGY
Mon. Jan. 9		
561	NYI	BUF
	at Minneapolis	
562	OTT	MTL
563	FLA	NYR
564	PIT	N.J.
	at Denver	
565	ANA	PHI
566	DAL	EDM
Tue. Jan. 10		
567	WPG	TOR
568	L.A.	ST.L.
569	T.B.	CGY
Wed. Jan. 11		
570	WSH	BUF
571	BOS	OTT
572	FLA	NYI
573	PIT	NYR
574	PHI	N.J.
575	ANA	DET
576	T.B.	EDM
577	CHI	VAN
578	DAL	S.J.

GAME #	VISITOR	HOME
Thur. Jan. 12		
579	WPG	BOS
580	MTL	QUE
581	FLA	PHI
582	ANA	TOR
583	CHI	CGY
584	ST.L.	L.A.
Fri. Jan. 13		
585	HFD	PIT
586	NYI	N.J.
587	WPG	DET
588	BUF	CGY
589	T.B.	VAN
Sat. Jan. 14		
590	NYI	PIT
591	FLA	MTL
592	BOS	QUE
593	OTT	PHI
594	NYR	WSH
595	DET	TOR
596	EDM	VAN
597	ST.L.	S.J.
598	DAL	L.A.
Sun. Jan. 15		
599	ANA	OTT
600	N.J.	NYR
601	HFD	CHI
602	T.B.	WPG
603	BUF	EDM
Mon. Jan. 16		
604	* WSH	BOS
605	* PHI	NYI
606	HFD	DAL
607	L.A.	CGY
608	VAN	S.J.

GAME #	VISITOR	HOME
Tue. Jan. 17		
609	ANA	QUE
610	DET	NYR
611	N.J.	FLA
612	CHI	TOR
613	ST.L.	WPG
614	L.A.	EDM
Wed. Jan. 18		
615	PIT	BOS
616	ANA	MTL
617	QUE	NYI
618	WSH	PHI
619	N.J.	T.B.
620	TOR	DET
621	DAL	HFD
	at Denver	
622	WPG	CGY
623	BUF	VAN
Sat. Jan. 21		
	All-Star Game	
	at San Jose	
Mon. Jan. 23		
624	PHI	PIT
625	OTT	BUF
626	HFD	MTL
627	QUE	NYR
628	T.B.	FLA
629	EDM	CGY
630	L.A.	S.J.
Tue. Jan. 24		
631	WSH	QUE
632	ST.L.	NYI
633	VAN	DET
634	DAL	L.A.

JANUARY 25 – FEBRUARY 8, 1995

GAME #	VISITOR	HOME
Wed. Jan. 25		
635	OTT	HFD
636	N.J.	BUF
637	BOS	NYR
638	CGY	T.B.
639	VAN	TOR
640	EDM	CHI
641	WPG	S.J.
642	DAL	ANA
Thur. Jan. 26		
643	N.J.	BOS
644	WSH	NYI
645	HFD	PHI
646	CGY	FLA
647	EDM	ST.L.
648	S.J.	L.A.
Fri. Jan. 27		
649	VAN	PIT
650	QUE	BUF
651	T.B.	NYR
652	OTT	WSH
653	TOR	CHI
654	WPG	ANA
Sat. Jan. 28		
655	* FLA	HFD
656	TOR	PIT
657	BUF	OTT
658	* N.J.	MTL
659	NYR	QUE
660	T.B.	NYI
661	* BOS	PHI
662	* EDM	DET
663	CGY	ST.L.
664	* DAL	S.J.
665	WPG	L.A.
Sun. Jan. 29		
666	* PHI	MTL
667	* CHI	WSH

GAME #	VISITOR	HOME
Mon. Jan. 30		
668	FLA	BOS
669	NYI	NYR
670	S.J.	TOR
671	DET	EDM
672	HFD	VAN
Tue. Jan. 31		
673	WSH	N.J.
674	CHI	PHI
675	NYI	FLA
676	ANA	ST.L.
677	WPG	L.A.
	at Phoenix	
Wed. Feb. 1		
678	S.J.	OTT
679	MTL	T.B.
680	DET	CGY
681	HFD	EDM
682	TOR	VAN
Thur. Feb. 2		
683	OTT	BOS
684	CHI	NYR
685	BUF	N.J.
686	NYI	PHI
687	QUE	WSH
688	MTL	FLA
689	L.A.	ST.L.
690	T.B.	DAL
691	PIT	WPG
Fri. Feb. 3		
692	HFD	CGY
693	TOR	EDM
694	DET	ANA

GAME #	VISITOR	HOME
Sat. Feb. 4		
695	* NYI	BOS
696	T.B.	PIT
697	NYR	OTT
698	VAN	MTL
699	* S.J.	QUE
700	* CHI	N.J.
701	* BUF	PHI
702	FLA	WSH
703	DAL	ST.L.
704	HFD	WPG
705	TOR	CGY
706	DET	L.A.
Sun. Feb. 5		
707	* N.J.	QUE
708	DAL	FLA
709	* EDM	ANA
Mon. Feb. 6		
710	VAN	OTT
711	S.J.	MTL
712	WPG	NYR
713	T.B.	DET
	at Hamilton	
714	EDM	L.A.
Tue. Feb. 7		
715	NYR	BOS
716	FLA	PIT
717	DAL	BUF
718	VAN	QUE
719	WPG	NYI
720	PHI	TOR
Wed. Feb. 8		
721	S.J.	HFD
722	MTL	OTT
723	L.A.	N.J.
724	WSH	T.B.
725	CHI	EDM
726	CGY	ANA

* – afternoon game

FEBRUARY 9 – 23, 1995

GAME #	VISITOR	HOME
Thur. Feb. 9		
727	S.J.	BOS
728	QUE	PIT
729	FLA	BUF
730	NYR	PHI
731	L.A.	DET
732	ST.L.	ANA
	at Las Vegas	
733	CHI	VAN
Fri. Feb. 10		
734	TOR	N.J.
735	WSH	PHI
	at Halifax	
736	HFD	T.B.
737	CGY	DAL
738	WPG	EDM
Sat. Feb. 11		
739	* L.A.	BOS
740	MTL	PIT
741	OTT	QUE
742	* S.J.	NYI
743	NYR	T.B.
744	HFD	FLA
745	BUF	TOR
746	CGY	ST.L.
747	DET	DAL
748	WPG	VAN
Sun. Feb. 12		
749	BOS	BUF
750	* N.J.	WSH
	at Halifax	
751	PIT	FLA
752	DET	ST.L.
753	* ANA	EDM
Mon. Feb. 13		
754	HFD	MTL
755	L.A.	PHI
756	NYI	T.B.
757	TOR	DAL
758	ANA	CGY
Tue. Feb. 14		
759	EDM	PIT
Wed. Feb. 15		
760	MTL	HFD
761	NYR	BUF
762	ST.L.	N.J.
763	T.B.	WSH
764	NYI	FLA
765	CHI	TOR
766	EDM	DET
767	BOS	DAL
768	CGY	WPG
769	OTT	S.J.
770	QUE	ANA
Thur. Feb. 16		
771	MTL	NYR
772	ST.L.	PHI
773	PIT	CHI
774	S.J.	VAN
775	QUE	L.A.
Fri. Feb. 17		
776	NYI	N.J.
777	BOS	T.B.
778	BUF	FLA
779	WSH	DET
780	DAL	WPG
781	OTT	ANA
Sat. Feb. 18		
782	* PIT	HFD
783	ST.L.	MTL
784	N.J.	NYI
785	* EDM	PHI
786	DET	WSH
787	BUF	T.B.
788	NYR	TOR
789	DAL	CGY
790	QUE	S.J.
791	OTT	L.A.
Sun. Feb. 19		
792	* HFD	PIT
793	BOS	FLA
794	* WPG	CHI
795	L.A.	ANA
Mon. Feb. 20		
796	WPG	BUF
797	* TOR	NYR
798	* MTL	WSH
799	NYI	DET
800	EDM	ST.L.
801	DAL	CGY
802	QUE	VAN
	at Saskatoon	
803	* PHI	S.J.
Tue. Feb. 21		
804	PIT	N.J.
805	OTT	CHI
806	ANA	L.A.
Wed. Feb. 22		
807	BOS	HFD
808	NYI	BUF
809	T.B.	DET
810	TOR	ST.L.
811	VAN	WPG
812	S.J.	CGY
	at Phoenix	
813	DAL	EDM
814	PHI	ANA
Thur. Feb. 23		
815	QUE	OTT
816	T.B.	N.J.
817	MTL	FLA
818	WSH	CHI
819	PHI	L.A.

FEBRUARY 24 – MARCH 10, 1995

GAME #	VISITOR	HOME
Fri. Feb. 24		
820	ST.L.	PIT
821	HFD	NYR
822	NYI	TOR
823	VAN	DAL
824	DET	WPG
825	ANA	S.J.
Sat. Feb. 25		
826	BUF	HFD
827	FLA	OTT
828	TOR	MTL
829	BOS	QUE
830	PIT	NYI
831	* WSH	N.J.
832	CHI	ST.L.
833	PHI	EDM
834	CGY	L.A.
Sun. Feb. 26		
835	NYR	BUF
836	* N.J.	WSH
837	DET	CHI
838	* T.B.	S.J.
839	* VAN	ANA
Mon. Feb. 27		
840	FLA	MTL
	at Hamilton	
841	ST.L.	TOR
Tue. Feb. 28		
842	QUE	BOS
843	S.J.	BUF
844	CHI	OTT
845	HFD	NYI
846	FLA	NYR
847	EDM	CGY
848	PIT	VAN
849	T.B.	L.A.

GAME #	VISITOR	HOME
Wed. Mar. 1		
850	N.J.	HFD
851	S.J.	TOR
852	OTT	DET
853	MTL	DAL
854	VAN	EDM
855	T.B.	ANA
Thur. Mar. 2		
856	N.J.	BOS
857	FLA	PHI
858	NYI	WSH
859	BUF	CHI
860	QUE	WPG
861	PIT	CGY
862	L.A.	ST.L.
	at Las Vegas	
Fri. Mar. 3		
863	PHI	NYR
864	TOR	DET
865	ANA	DAL
866	PIT	EDM
Sat. Mar. 4		
867	* OTT	BOS
868	* CHI	HFD
869	BUF	QUE
870	NYR	NYI
871	* FLA	N.J.
872	S.J.	WSH
873	CGY	TOR
874	* ST.L.	WPG
875	MTL	L.A.
Sun. Mar. 5		
876	BOS	HFD
877	CGY	BUF
878	NYI	OTT
879	S.J.	PHI
880	ANA	FLA
881	* ST.L.	CHI
882	* DET	EDM

GAME #	VISITOR	HOME
Mon. Mar. 6		
883	PIT	QUE
884	N.J.	NYR
885	ANA	T.B.
886	L.A.	DAL
887	DET	VAN
Tue. Mar. 7		
888	N.J.	NYI
889	CGY	WSH
890	WPG	CHI
891	OTT	ST.L.
Wed. Mar. 8		
892	PHI	HFD
893	WSH	MTL
894	BUF	NYR
895	QUE	FLA
896	DAL	WPG
897	EDM	S.J.
Thur. Mar. 9		
898	QUE	PIT
899	MTL	NYI
900	CGY	PHI
901	BOS	T.B.
	at Minneapolis	
902	L.A.	TOR
903	CHI	OTT
	at Phoenix	
904	HFD	ST.L.
905	EDM	VAN
906	DET	ANA
Fri. Mar. 10		
907	FLA	WSH
908	BUF	WPG
909	DET	S.J.

* – afternoon game

MARCH 11 – 25, 1995

GAME #	VISITOR	HOME
Sat. Mar. 11		
910	* CGY	PIT
911	NYR	MTL
912	NYI	QUE
913	PHI	T.B.
914	N.J.	TOR
915	L.A.	WPG
916	OTT	VAN
917	ANA	DAL
	at San Antonio	
Sun. Mar. 12		
918	* BOS	WSH
919	DET	FLA
	at Denver	
920	* CGY	CHI
921	BUF	ST.L.
922	OTT	EDM
923	* HFD	S.J.
Mon. Mar. 13		
924	WPG	PIT
925	NYR	PHI
926	WSH	T.B.
927	TOR	DAL
Tue. Mar. 14		
928	BUF	BOS
	at Hamilton	
929	QUE	N.J.
930	CHI	DET
931	ST.L.	EDM
932	NYI	VAN
933	HFD	L.A.
Wed. Mar. 15		
934	WPG	MTL
935	N.J.	NYR
936	WSH	FLA
937	PHI	DAL
938	OTT	CGY
939	TOR	S.J.
940	HFD	ANA

GAME #	VISITOR	HOME
Thur. Mar. 16		
941	MTL	BOS
942	T.B.	PIT
943	DET	BUF
944	WPG	QUE
945	VAN	CHI
946	ST.L.	L.A.
Fri. Mar. 17		
947	VAN	DET
948	S.J.	CGY
949	NYI	EDM
950	TOR	ANA
Sat. Mar. 18		
951	* BUF	BOS
952	HFD	CHI
	at Phoenix	
953	* PIT	OTT
954	DAL	MTL
955	* T.B.	N.J.
956	NYR	WSH
957	PHI	FLA
958	TOR	L.A.
Sun. Mar. 19		
959	* T.B.	BUF
960	DAL	OTT
961	* PIT	QUE
962	BOS	N.J.
963	* S.J.	WPG
964	NYI	CGY
965	* ST.L.	ANA
Mon. Mar. 20		
966	MTL	PHI
967	TOR	EDM
	at Saskatoon	
968	FLA	L.A.

GAME #	VISITOR	HOME
Tue. Mar. 21		
969	PIT	BUF
970	OTT	WSH
971	NYR	DAL
972	DET	CGY
973	N.J.	EDM
974	ST.L.	VAN
975	CHI	S.J.
976	FLA	ANA
Wed. Mar. 22		
977	QUE	HFD
978	BOS	MTL
979	OTT	T.B.
980	DET	WPG
Thur. Mar. 23		
981	PHI	NYI
982	CGY	NYR
	at Phoenix	
983	ANA	ST.L.
984	EDM	DAL
985	N.J.	VAN
986	FLA	S.J.
987	CHI	L.A.
Fri. Mar. 24		
988	MTL	PIT
989	QUE	BUF
990	BOS	T.B.
991	WPG	TOR
992	N.J.	CGY
Sat. Mar. 25		
993	* NYI	HFD
994	BUF	MTL
995	OTT	QUE
996	* ANA	WSH
997	TOR	WPG
998	DET	VAN
999	* S.J.	L.A.

MARCH 26 – APRIL 9, 1995

GAME #	VISITOR	HOME
Sun. Mar. 26		
1000	EDM	OTT
1001	* ANA	NYI
1002	PIT	PHI
1003	* HFD	WSH
1004	T.B.	FLA
1005	* DAL	CHI
1006	BOS	ST.L.
1007	VAN	CGY
1008	* L.A.	S.J.
Mon. Mar. 27		
1009	MTL	T.B.
1010	EDM	TOR
1011	CHI	DAL
Tue. Mar. 28		
1012	NYI	BOS
1013	PHI	PIT
1014	ST.L.	QUE
1015	NYR	DET
1016	WPG	S.J.
Wed. Mar. 29		
1017	EDM	BUF
1018	ST.L.	OTT
1019	WSH	T.B.
1020	HFD	FLA
1021	DAL	TOR
1022	DET	CHI
1023	L.A.	VAN
1024	WPG	ANA
Thur. Mar. 30		
1025	BOS	PIT
1026	MTL	NYI
1027	QUE	NYR
1028	N.J.	PHI

GAME #	VISITOR	HOME
Fri. Mar. 31		
1029	PHI	WSH
1030	HFD	T.B.
1031	QUE	CHI
1032	TOR	ST.L.
1033	S.J.	CGY
1034	L.A.	EDM
1035	ANA	VAN
Sat. Apr. 1		
1036	* NYR	BOS
1037	* BUF	NYI
1038	MTL	N.J.
1039	* DET	DAL
1040	WPG	L.A.
Sun. Apr. 2		
1041	* OTT	BUF
1042	* NYI	QUE
1043	* BOS	PHI
1044	* FLA	T.B.
1045	* PIT	TOR
1046	* ST.L.	DET
1047	* NYR	CHI
1048	* WSH	DAL
1049	* CGY	VAN
1050	* S.J.	ANA
Mon. Apr. 3		
1051	MTL	OTT
1052	EDM	L.A.
Tue. Apr. 4		
1053	PHI	BOS
1054	ST.L.	BUF
1055	PIT	NYI
1056	HFD	N.J.
1057	DAL	VAN

GAME #	VISITOR	HOME
Wed. Apr. 5		
1058	TOR	HFD
1059	N.J.	PIT
1060	QUE	MTL
1061	WSH	NYR
1062	OTT	FLA
1063	CHI	WPG
1064	CGY	S.J.
1065	EDM	ANA
Thur. Apr. 6		
1066	MTL	QUE
1067	BOS	NYI
1068	T.B.	PHI
1069	TOR	CHI
1070	DET	ST.L.
1071	VAN	L.A.
Fri. Apr. 7		
1072	WSH	BUF
1073	OTT	NYR
1074	FLA	WPG
1075	L.A.	CGY
1076	EDM	S.J.
1077	DAL	ANA
Sat. Apr. 8		
1078	* T.B.	BOS
1079	* N.J.	HFD
1080	QUE	OTT
1081	PIT	MTL
1082	BUF	WSH
1083	DET	TOR
1084	VAN	CGY
Sun. Apr. 9		
1085	* T.B.	HFD
1086	* NYR	N.J.
1087	* BOS	CHI
1088	* PHI	ST.L.
1089	* FLA	DAL
1090	* NYI	WPG
1091	S.J.	EDM
1092	* L.A.	ANA

NHL STARTING TIMES, 1994-95

(All Times are Local)

ANAHEIM

Weeknights.................... 7:30 p.m.
Sundays........................ 5:00 p.m.
Matinees........................ 1:00 p.m.
Except
- Fri. Dec. 16................ 6:00 p.m.
- Mon. Jan. 2............. 11:00 a.m.
- Sun. Apr. 2, Apr. 9..... 12:00 p.m.
- Wed. Apr. 5............... 8:00 p.m.
- Fri. Apr. 7................ 8:00 p.m.

BOSTON

Weeknights.................... 7:30 p.m.
Saturdays and Sundays....... 7:00 p.m.
Matinees........................ 1:30 p.m.
Except
- Sat. Oct. 8................ 7:30 p.m.
- Fri. Nov. 25............... 1:00 p.m.

BUFFALO

Tuesdays through Saturdays... 7:30 p.m.
Sundays and Mondays.......... 7:00 p.m.
Matinees........................ 2:00 p.m.

CALGARY

Weeknights.................... 7:30 p.m.
Saturdays...................... 8:30 p.m.
Sundays........................ 6:00 p.m.
Except Sat. Dec. 31........... 5:30 p.m.

CHICAGO

Night Games.................... 7:30 p.m.
Matinees........................ 1:30 p.m.
Except
- Sun. Jan. 8, Feb. 26...... 7:00 p.m.
- Sun. Apr. 2, Apr. 9...... 12:00 p.m.

DALLAS

Weeknights...................... 7:30 p.m.
Saturday and Sunday nights..... 7:00 p.m.
Saturday matinees............... 1:00 p.m.
Sunday matinees................. 12:00 p.m.

DETROIT

Night Games.................... 7:30 p.m.
Matinees........................ 1:00 p.m.

EDMONTON

Weeknights.................... 7:30 p.m.
Saturdays...................... 8:30 p.m.
Sundays........................ 6:00 p.m.
Matinees........................ 2:00 p.m.

FLORIDA

Weeknights.................... 7:30 p.m.
Saturday nights................. 7:30 p.m.
Saturday matinees.............. 1:00 p.m.
Sunday nights................... 6:00 p.m.
Sunday matinees............... 12:00 p.m.
Except
- Sat. Dec. 10............... 7:00 p.m.
- Sun. Feb. 5................ 8:00 p.m.
- Sun. Mar. 5................ 7:30 p.m.

HARTFORD

Night Games.................... 7:00 p.m.
Matinees........................ 1:30 p.m.

LOS ANGELES

Night Games.................... 7:30 p.m.
Matinees........................ 1:00 p.m.

MONTREAL

Night Games.................... 7:30 p.m.
Matinees........................ 1:30 p.m.

NEW JERSEY

Night Games.................... 7:30 p.m.
Matinees........................ 1:00 p.m.
Except Sun. Mar. 19........... 8:00 p.m.

NEW YORK ISLANDERS

Weeknights.................... 7:30 p.m.
Saturday and Sunday nights... 7:00 p.m.
Matinees....................... 1:00 p.m.
Except
- Sat. Nov. 26............... 7:30 p.m.
- Mon. Jan. 16.............. 1:00 p.m.

NHL STARTING TIMES

continued

NEW YORK RANGERS

Weeknights......................7:30 p.m.
Sundays..........................7:00 p.m.
Except
Sun. Jan. 15...............8:00 p.m.
Mon. Feb. 20..............1:30 p.m.

OTTAWA

Mondays through Saturdays..... 7:30 p.m.
Sundays......................... 7:00 p.m.
Matinees.........................1:30 p.m.

PHILADELPHIA

Mondays through Saturdays..... 7:30 p.m.
Sundays......................... 7:00 p.m.
Matinees.........................1:00 p.m.
Except
Wed. Dec. 21..............7:00 p.m.
Sat. Feb. 4.................12:00 p.m.
Thu. Feb 9, Mar. 2........7:00 p.m.
Sun. Mar. 26...............8:00 p.m.

PITTSBURGH

Night Games....................7:30 p.m.
Matinees......................... 1:30 p.m.
Except Sat. Dec. 31........... 6:30 p.m.

QUEBEC

Weeknights......................7:30 p.m.
Saturdays...................... 7:00 p.m.
Matinees.........................1:30 p.m.
Except Sat. Jan. 28............7:30 p.m.

ST. LOUIS

Mondays through Saturdays..... 7:30 p.m.
Sundays.......................... 6:00 p.m.
Matinees........................12:00 p.m.
Except
Sat. Oct. 22............... 6:30 p.m.
Sun. Feb. 12...............7:00 p.m.

SAN JOSE

Night Games....................7:30 p.m.
Matinees......................... 2:00 p.m.
Except Fri. Oct. 7.............. 6:00 p.m.

TAMPA BAY

Night Games....................7:30 p.m.
Matinees......................... 1:00 p.m.

TORONTO

Night Games....................7:30 p.m.
Matinees......................... 1:30 p.m.
Except
Sat. Dec. 31...............5:00 p.m.

VANCOUVER

Night Games....................7:30 p.m.
Matinees......................... 2:00 p.m.
Except
Sat. Dec. 31...............5:00 p.m.

WASHINGTON

Mondays through Thursdays..... 7:30 p.m.
Fridays.......................... 8:00 p.m.
Saturdays........................7:30 p.m.
Matinees.........................1:30 p.m.
Except
Fri. Oct. 14............... 7:30 p.m.
Sat. Nov. 5.................7:00 p.m.
Wed. Nov. 23............ 8:00 p.m.
Fri. Nov. 25............... 7:30 p.m.
Sun. Jan. 29............. 12:00 p.m.

WINNIPEG

Weeknights..................... 7:30 p.m.
Saturdays and Sundays....... 6:30 p.m.
Matinees.........................2:00 p.m.
Except
Sat. Dec. 31...............4:30 p.m.
Sun. Mar. 19..............1:00 p.m.

The
NHL
also
publishes

The NHL Official Guide & Record Book

This is the same book used by broadcasters and reporters when covering hockey

•

An excellent gift for any hockey fan

•

Available at your local book store or by mail

•

To order your copy by mail, please complete the form on the following page

NHL PUBLICATIONS
ORDER FORM

Please send

☐ copies of the *NHL Guide & Record Book/94-95 (available now)*

☐ copies of the *NHL Guide & Record Book/95-96 (available Sept. 95)*

PRICES:	**CANADA**	**U.S.A.**	**OVERSEAS**
Guide & Record Book	$19.95	$16.95	$19.95 CDN
Postage (per copy)	$3.88	$8.00	$9.00 CDN
7% GST	$1.67	–	–
Total (per copy)	**$25.50**	**$24.95**	**$28.95 CDN**
Add Extra for airmail	$8.00	$9.00	$18.00 CDN

☐ Enclosed is my cheque or money order.

Charge my ☐ Visa ☐ MasterCard ☐ Am Ex

Credit Card Expiry Date (important)

Signature

Name

Address

Province/State Postal/Zip Code

IN CANADA

Mail completed form to:

NHL Publishing
194 Dovercourt Rd.
Toronto, Ontario
M6J 3C8

IN U.S.A.

Mail completed form to:

NHL Publishing
194 Dovercourt Rd.
Toronto, Ontario
M6J 3C8

Remit in U.S. funds

OVERSEAS

Mail completed form to:

NHL Publishing
194 Dovercourt Rd.
Toronto, Ontario
CANADA M6J 3C8

Money order or credit card only
No cheques, please

Please allow up to five weeks for delivery.